Gulf-Asia
Energy Security

Edited by
John Calabrese

The Middle East Institute
Washington, DC

Table of Contents

Appendix

Contributors

Acknowledgments

The Middle East Institute is grateful for the financial support of the W. Alton Jones Foundation for our conference and edited monograph on "Gulf-Asia Energy Security." Special thanks are due to MEI scholar-in-residence Dr. John Calabrese, who conceived the project, served as project director, and edited this volume. Thanks are also due to MEI program officer Mohammed Khraishah for his valuable suggestions and deft handling of the logistical arrangements for the conference. MEI editorial assistant Leslie Hunter deserves credit for her skillful design and layout of this book. Finally, MEI thanks the authors for their contributions.

Roscoe S. Suddarth
President
The Middle East Institute

Introduction

John Calabrese

For the Persian Gulf and Asia-Pacific regions, the period 1980-96 was one of sharply contrasting trends: revolutionary upheaval and war in the former and unprecedented high rates of economic growth in the latter. Despite persistent conflict in the Persian Gulf and primarily because of the rapid and sustained expansion of the Asian "tiger" economies, Asian consumption of oil from the Gulf rose dramatically.

Although the growth of Gulf-Asia oil ties introduces the possibility of shared prosperity and interstate cooperation, it also poses risks. In a climate of regional rivalry or warfare, will governments use oil as a weapon? How will they manage market-driven or conflict-driven supply disruptions? Self-help and military means constitute one set of approaches to these challenges. Cooperative non-military efforts to anticipate, forestall, or minimize these problems represent another. These issues are of great importance to the United States, which has major defense commitments and vital economic interests in both regions.

The chapters in this volume examine Gulf-Asia energy interdependence, focusing on the links between energy and security. The first section, consisting of chapters by Fadhil Chalabi and John Mitchell, explores the substance and scope of Gulf-Asia energy ties and the prospects for their further development. Both Chalabi and Mitchell argue that Gulf-Asia energy interdependence is a structural feature of the world energy market. Chalabi explains why the Asia-Pacific region has emerged as the Persian Gulf's main market for crude oil. He presents two scenarios concerning Asia's economic recovery and the resumption of growth in Asian demand for Middle Eastern oil. Mitchell, like Chalabi, argues that the trade of crude oil is the core element of an increasingly complex web of energy ties between the Gulf and Asia-Pacific regions. He differentiates among the Asia-Pacific countries in terms of the extent of their oil import dependence on the Gulf, as well as in terms of the impact of their current economic and political problems on energy relations with the Gulf states. Mitchell identifies "policy gaps" which, at the national level, have constrained the joint development of upstream and downstream energy projects, and which, at the regional level, could complicate the management of future oil supply disruptions.

The second section, composed of chapters by Yang Guang, Sujit Dutta, and Katsuhiko Suetsugu, examines the links between energy and geopolitics from the Asian perspective. Guang discusses the imbalance between energy demand and energy production in China, which is responsible for that country's increasing reliance on imported oil, especially from the Gulf. He argues that China's rising dependence on Middle Eastern oil has reinforced its commitment to maintain friendly and "balanced" relations with the Gulf countries and to support non-military approaches to regional security problems. Like Guang's depiction of China's expanding involvement in the Gulf, Dutta portrays India's activities there as non-threatening. Yet, Dutta argues, India's energy ties to the Gulf cannot be separated from the social and political dimensions of Indo-Gulf relations, nor from the geopolitical situation in South Asia. Dutta discusses how these considerations have shaped India's policy toward the Gulf. Suetsugu frames his discussion of Gulf-Asia energy ties in terms of East Asian energy policy and power politics. He points out that the possible liberalization of the petroleum products market in Japan will create opportunities for broader Gulf-Asia energy interdependence. Whereas Suetsugu doubts that any Asian country can or will project force into the Gulf in the foreseeable future, he is less sanguine about the likelihood of, and the dangers posed by, arms transfers to the Gulf by some Asian countries, notably North Korea.

The chapters that comprise the third section also deal with the interplay between energy and geopolitics, but they are written from a Gulf perspective. Narsi Ghorban discusses Iran's role as an energy supplier to the South and East Asian markets. He argues that Iran's potential to serve these markets can be maximized by exploiting its proximity to Central Asian oil and gas fields. Ghorban maintains that the development of an Iran-Central Asia energy corridor will be not only commercially profitable, but also security-enhancing. Issam Al-Chalabi argues that past fears about oil supply security based on predictions of supply scarcity proved unfounded. He contends that the Gulf countries will remain residual producers for decades to come. According to Al-Chalabi, this will ensure that the Gulf, including Iraq, retains its geopolitical importance for Asia-Pacific countries and others with economic interests in the region.

The final set of chapters deals with the implications for US policy of growing Gulf-Asia energy interdependence. Geoffrey Kemp identifies the security risks that these energy ties might pose for the United States.

He also emphasizes the opportunities that they create for the United States to consider how to fulfill its long-term security responsibility in the Gulf and how to promote regional efforts for managing potential oil supply disruptions. Patrick Cronin considers five scenarios in which growing Gulf-Asia oil ties might contribute to regional tension or conflict, thereby posing policy challenges for the United States: expanded economic competition; transportation of oil as a force-building justification; arms-for-oil arrangements; opposition to the US security role; and economic depression in Asia.

Notwithstanding differences in emphasis and approach, the contributors to this volume reach several common conclusions regarding Gulf-Asia energy ties and their possible security implications. First, Asia's dependence on oil from the Gulf and position as the Gulf's main market for oil exports are irreversible structural features of the world energy market. Second, the energy policies of Asia-Pacific countries are of great importance to the Gulf states, which seek to acquire a strategic foothold in the Asian energy market, particularly in downstream industries. Third, Asia-Pacific countries must establish, but have yet to explore fully, multilateral mechanisms to manage potential oil supply disruptions. Fourth, Asia-Pacific powers appear to have neither the immediate capacity nor any specific plans to project their forces into the Gulf; and, with the possible exception of North Korea, they do not seem strongly inclined to enter arms-for-oil arrangements with the Gulf states. Finally, the contributors to this volume agree that it is essential for US policymakers and others to consider building new multi-level, multi-dimensional regional security frameworks that progressively lessen or eliminate the need for a large Western military presence, and that incorporate non-military elements, encompass the interests and concerns of the Gulf and Asia-Pacific countries, and depend, in fact, on their contributions and cooperation.

Energy and the Economy

Gulf-Asia Energy Interdependence

Fadhil Chalabi

The Asian financial crisis has triggered a world-wide debate not only about future oil supply and demand, but also about the future price of oil. The impact and implications of this crisis on Gulf oil-producing countries are far-reaching, but should not be overstated. Prior to the crisis, the Asia-Pacific region had already emerged as the leading energy market for Gulf producers. In 1996, 63 percent of their oil exports went to Asia, including Japan. Economic recovery and the resumption of economic growth in the Asia-Pacific region are vitally important to the stability and prosperity of the Gulf.

The Recent Pattern of Asia-Pacific Oil Demand

In recent years, the ten Asian "tiger" economies have propelled the growth of world oil demand. Over the period 1986-96, global oil demand (excluding the former Soviet Union and Eastern Europe) rose by 14.1 million barrels per day (mb/d). During this period, the combined oil demand of the Asian tigers accounted for no less than 41 percent of this growth. Asian oil demand grew at an average annual rate of 7.3 percent, the same rate at which it declined in the former Soviet Union (FSU). The volume of oil consumed by Asia rose from 5.9 mb/d in 1986 to 12.1 mb/d in 1996. Thus, between 1986 and 1996, Asia experienced the highest oil demand growth of any region, both in percentage terms and in terms of volume. [See Table 1.] If demand were to continue rising at these high rates, Asia's oil consumption would surpass that of the United States by the year 2003.

The sharp increase in Asian oil demand was fueled by high rates of economic growth across the region. This growth was stimulated by industrial expansion and aided by the process of globalization. For most of the Asian tiger economies, the period 1985-95 was one of energy-intensive development. Accordingly, the demand for electricity grew exceptionally fast in the Asia-Pacific region during this time. Electricity demand grew at an annual rate of nearly 14 percent in Indonesia, over 12 percent in Thailand, and between 11-12 percent in Malaysia and South Korea. On the whole, electricity demand growth rates in Asia-Pacific

13

Table 1
Global Oil Demand* by Main Consuming Region

	1986	1996	Δ mbpd p.a.	Δ % p.a.
Period 1986-96				
USA & Canada	18.1	20.3	0.22	1.2
W. Europe	12.6	14.3	0.17	1.3
E. Europe	1.5	1.2	-0.03	-2.0
Japan+Aus/NZ	5.2	6.7	0.15	2.5
FSU	8.9	4.3	-0.46	-7.3
Asia	5.9	12.1	0.63	7.3
Latin America	4.9	6.3	0.15	2.6
Middle East	3.0	4.2	0.12	3.4
Africa	1.7	2.2	0.05	2.6
TOTAL	**61.8**	**71.6**	**1.00**	**1.29**
OECD	35.9	41.3	0.54	1.4

* In millions of barrels per day (mbpd) and per annum (p.a.)
Source: International Energy Agency (IEA), Paris, 1997.

countries were much higher than in industrialized countries.

Oil played a crucial role in the industrialization of the Asian tiger economies. The prominence of oil was due to the fact that it is an easily transportable and versatile primary energy source and that oil was comparatively cheap at the time. Oil's special role in the region's industrialization is evident in the relatively high shares of fuel oil and relatively low shares of gasoline in the fuel mix. In 1986, fuel oil constituted a 31 percent share of the fuel mix for Asian emerging market economies (EMEs), compared with 10 percent for the United States, 9 percent for Canada, and 20 percent for the OECD European countries. At that time, gasoline comprised 15 percent of the fuel mix for Asian EMEs, compared with 42 percent for the United States, 41 percent for Canada, and 24 percent for the OECD European countries. By the year 1996, the share of fuel oil had dropped to 26 percent, while that of gasoline had risen to 20 percent, for Asian EMEs. These changes reveal the structural transformation of the Asian EMEs towards economic maturity, that is, towards greater concentration in services.

Future Oil Demand in the Asia-Pacific Region

Whether the Asian financial crisis represents a fundamental structural change or a temporary phenomenon is debated widely. In order to project future oil demand in the Asia-Pacific region, one must first address this issue. The position taken here is that many of the Asian tiger

Table 2
Forecasts of Incremental Annual Demand* in the Asia-Pacific Region

	Period 1986-96 tbpd	Years 1995-96 tbpd	Forecasts for period 1994-2010		
			Business as usual tbpd	Reference case tbpd	Ultra low growth tbpd
India	70	115	51	53	40
Indonesia	44	75	45	40	26
S. Korea	156	135	153	93	53
Taiwan	33	0	49	34	19
Thailand	55	70	52	31	21
Malaysia	20	15	26	19	17
Philippines	20	15	7	6	5
Singapore	25	-5	21	17	9
Hong Kong	7	6	8	5	4
China	161	235	304	236	108
Total	**591**	**661**	**716**	**534**	**302**

* In thousands of barrels per day (tbpd)
Source: Centre for Global Energy Studies (CGES), London, 1997.

economies have attained economic maturity. In South Korea in particular, evidence clearly indicates that this is the case: investments have begun to shift into sectors which are comparatively less energy intensive.

The forecast for oil demand in the Asia-Pacific region that follows is based on four assumptions. First, the price of crude oil will continue to weaken until the early years of the next century, and will rise steadily thereafter. Second, taxes on oil products, which are currently low in Asia-Pacific countries, will rise in the coming years. Third, per capita Gross Domestic Product (GDP) growth in these countries will slow down and will certainly be lower than during the period 1985-95. Fourth, the rates of population growth in Asia-Pacific countries, which have already declined, will continue to do so. The net effect of these changes will be downward pressure on oil demand growth in the Asia-Pacific region.

Table 2 forecasts incremental annual oil demand in the Asia-Pacific region for the period 1994-2010. The "business as usual" scenario projects demand at 716,000 b/d. Yet, it is inconceivable that demand will attain this level, for it assumes economic growth rates that are unlikely to be replicated and energy-intensive development profiles that have begun to change as service sectors have expanded. The past will not be repeated. There are, however, two more realistic scenarios: the "reference" case, in

Table 3
Forecasts of Oil Demand* in the Asia-Pacific Region

	1996	Period 1986-96	Business as usual		Reference case		Ultra low growth	
			Forecasts for year 2010 & period 1994-2010					
	mbpd	% p.a.	mbpd	% p.a.	mbpd	% p.a.	mbpd	% p.a.
India	1.65	5.6	2.6	3.7	2.6	3.7	2.2	2.7
Indonesia	0.95	6.6	1.9	5.2	1.7	4.7	1.4	3.2
S. Korea	2.06	12.9	5.2	6.7	3.8	4.7	2.7	2.7
Taiwan	0.71	6.1	1.8	6.3	1.4	4.9	1.0	2.8
Thailand	0.75	11.9	1.7	6.7	1.3	4.7	1.0	3.3
Malaysia	0.41	7.1	1.0	5.9	0.8	4.9	0.8	4.5
Philippines	0.33	8.1	0.4	2.5	0.4	2.2	0.4	1.8
Singapore	0.30	6.5	0.7	5.8	0.7	5.0	0.5	2.9
Hong Kong	0.16	5.6	0.4	5.2	0.3	3.3	0.2	2.2
China	3.62	5.9	11.4	8.0	8.5	6.2	5.4	3.4
Total	**10.94**	**7.63**	**27.1**	**5.6**	**21.5**	**4.43**	**15.6**	**2.95**

* In millions of barrels per day (mbpd) and per annum (p.a.)
Source: CGES, London, 1997.

which Asia's annual incremental oil demand growth is projected at more than 500,000 b/d; and the "ultra low growth" case, in which this growth is projected at about 300,000 b/d.

As previously stated, the structural changes in the Asian tiger economies will constrain oil demand growth. It is therefore improbable that, by the year 2010, Asian demand will reach or surpass 27.1 mb/d, the figure given for the "business as usual" scenario in Table 3. Instead, Asian oil consumption will fall somewhere between 15.6 mb/d and 21.5 mb/d, as shown in the "ultra low growth" and "reference case" scenarios. Using these figures as the high and low estimates of Asian oil demand for the year 2010, one can expect Asian consumption to rise between 8-14 mb/d in the intervening time. This is more than Saudi Arabia's current total production. Thus, no matter how pessimistic the outlook for oil demand growth in Asia, the region's consumption of oil will certainly be much higher in the coming decades than it is today.

Not only will Asia's consumption of oil grow, but so will its net oil imports. [See Table 4.] In 1996, Asia's net oil imports (excluding Japan) were 5.4 mb/d, compared with 8.9 mb/d for all of Europe and 7.3 mb/d for the United States and Canada. Assuming an Asian oil demand growth rate higher than that of the "reference" case and lower than that of the "ultra low growth" case, Asia's net oil imports will reach 13.4 mb/d in the year 2010, while those of Europe will reach 11.0 mb/d and those of the United

Table 4
Net Oil Imports* by Region in 2010

	Demand (mbpd)		Changes 1996-2010		Supply	Net imports (+) in mbpd	
	2010	1996	Δ mbpd p.a.	Δ % p.a.	mbpd	1996	2010
USA & Canada	22.8	20.3	0.18	0.8	8.5	7.8	14.3
W. Europe	15.4	14.3	0.08	0.5	Europe:	Europe:	Europe:
E. Europe	2.1	1.2	0.06	3.8	6.5	8.9	11.0
Japan + Aus/NZ	7.3	6.7	0.04	0.6	0.8	5.8	6.5
FSU	5.5	4.3	0.09	1.8	9.8	-3.2	-4.3
Asia	19.6	12.1	0.53	3.4	6.2	5.4	13.4
Latin America	9.2	6.3	0.20	2.7	13.7	-3.1	-4.5
Middle East	4.6	4.2	0.03	0.7	34.8	-16.9	-30.2
Africa	3.3	2.2	0.08	2.8	9.5	-4.7	-6.2
Total	**89.8**	**71.6**	**1.29**	**1.9**	**89.8**	**0**	**0**
OECD	45.5	41.3	0.30	0.7			

* In millions of barrels per day (mbpd) and per annum (p.a.)
Source: CGES, London, 1997.

States and Canada will reach 14.3 mb/d. As the next section will show, the future growth of Asia's oil consumption, and of its net imports, is of great significance to Gulf oil-producing countries.

The Asia-Pacific Region and Gulf Oil

The Middle East (especially the Gulf) is the world's largest oil-exporting area. This region is the primary source of Asia-Pacific countries' oil imports. In 1996, 87 percent of Asian oil imports (excluding Japan's) originated from the Middle East. By the year 2010, Asia-Pacific countries (including Japan) will obtain nearly all of their oil imports from this region. [See Table 5.] Thus, in the coming years, the Gulf will be an even more important source of Asian oil imports than it has been. Meanwhile, the United States will become somewhat more, and Europe somewhat less, dependent on oil imports from the Middle East than they are today.

In 1984, crude oil from the Gulf had already constituted just over 50 percent of Asia's total oil imports. By 1996, Asia's dependence on oil imports from the Gulf had risen to as high as 70 percent. [See Graph 1.] From the point of view of Gulf oil exporters, Asia will continue to be a vital market. Over the period 1996-2010, the share of the Middle East's oil exports going to the Asia-Pacific region as a whole is expected to rise from 63 to 66 percent. [See Table 6.] In contrast, by the year 2010, North

Table 5*
Oil Import Shares (%): Comparison of 1996 to 2010

2010	FSU	L. Amer.	M. East	Africa	Europe	Asia	Total
N. America	0	32	40	28	0	0	100
Europe	39	0	41	20	0	0	100
Japan + Aus/NZ	0	0	100	0	0	0	100
Asia	0	0	100	0	0	0	100
1996	**FSU**	**L. Amer.**	**M. East**	**Africa**	**Europe**	**Asia**	**Total**
N. America	0	45	20	19	13	3	100
Europe	26	4	39	31	0	0	100
Japan + Aus/NZ	0	2	76	1	0	22	100
Asia	2	1	87	6	3	0	100

* Due to rounding, totals may not equal 100 percent.
Source: CGES, London, 1997.

Graph 1
Asia's Dependence on Crude Oil Imports from Gulf OPEC (%)

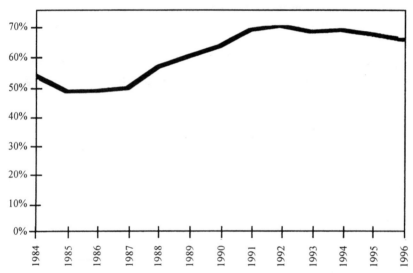

Source: CGES, London, 1997.

America and Europe will constitute only 19 percent and 15 percent, respectively, of the Middle East oil export market. The Asia-Pacific region will therefore continue to be the main market outlet for Gulf oil.

Interdependence between the Asia-Pacific and Gulf regions in the oil sector is firmly entrenched. From the Gulf perspective, Asian oil imports from the Gulf will remain a crucial factor in sustaining economic growth in the Gulf. This is true because of the heavy dependence of the Gulf economies on oil and the large share Asia occupies in Gulf countries' overall exports. Gulf oil-exporting countries and their Asia-Pacific

Table 6*
Oil Export Shares (%): Comparison of 1996 to 2010

Importers	Exporters					
2010	FSU	L. Amer.	M. East	Africa	Europe	Asia
N. America	0	100	19	65	0	0
Europe	100	0	15	35	0	0
Japan + Aus/NZ	0	0	22	0	0	0
Asia	0	0	44	0	0	0
Total	100	100	100	100	0	0
1996	FSU	L. Amer.	M. East	Africa	Europe	Asia
N. America	1	87	11	30	82	17
Europe	92	8	23	56	0	3
Japan + Aus/ NZ	0	2	26	1	0	78
Asia	5	2	37	8	15	0
L. America	2	0	3	6	3	3
Total	100	100	100	100	100	100

*Due to rounding, totals may not equal 100 percent.
Source: CGES, London, 1997.

customers have a common interest in developing additional economic ties. One potentially fruitful area of Gulf-Asia economic cooperation is downstream activities. By the year 2010, the Asia-Pacific region will require about 18 mb/d of oil, or about 400-500,000 b/d per year more than the region's present consumption. To accommodate this increase, Asian countries must expand their refining capacity. In fact, they will have to add about 250,000 b/d in new refining capacity each year. This will require a considerable financial outlay. Using this as an opportunity to strengthen the economic interdependence between the two regions, Gulf oil producers should invest in the construction and expansion of refineries in Asia.

Asia's Stake in the Security of Supply

In the coming years, energy interdependence between the Gulf and Asia-Pacific countries will continue to increase. This will not just entail, but may in fact require, closer political and economic links between the two regions. Asia will remain the leading market outlet for Gulf oil, thus sustaining the Gulf's economic growth. Meanwhile, the continuation of Asia's industrial expansion will depend on secure oil supplies from the Gulf at reasonably stable prices.

The security of oil supplies from the Gulf is of general concern to the world economy, given the importance of oil price stability. This can only be guaranteed through the uninterrupted flow of oil from this prolific oil-bearing region. The "new realities" of the world oil market suggest that the issue of security of oil supplies is no longer exclusively a strategic concern of the West. Asia's stake in securing reliable oil supplies is even greater because of the relative increase in its degree of dependence on oil from the Gulf.

The expression "security of supply" was first evoked in 1956 following the closure of the Suez Canal. This led to sudden and substantial increases in freight rates, due to the shortage of small tankers and the transportation costs for larger tankers taking the longer route around the Cape. It also led to higher oil prices in Europe and more US oil exports to Europe to fill the gap. In response, Western countries tried to diversify their sources of supply by intensifying oil exploration outside the Gulf region, especially in Africa.

The oil shocks of the 1970s reinforced this need to diversify. These crises led to the adoption of new measures and policies: oil exploration in the North Sea and Latin America; greater diversification of the energy mix; increased reliance on domestic energy sources; greater efficiency of fuel utilization through conservation and lower oil intensity; the establishment of strategic stockpiles; and military policing.

Asian countries must anticipate and plan to cope with possible future oil shocks. However, Asian countries do not have the same flexibility of diversification as their European counterparts. With respect to diversifying their sources of imported energy, Asian countries are limited by geography. The neighboring countries of the former Soviet Union, especially those bordering the Caspian Sea, have the energy resources that might relieve the Asia-Pacific region's dependence on Gulf oil. Yet, these resources might take years to develop, given high transportation costs, not to mention political and geopolitical obstacles.

On the whole, Asian countries face greater constraints than their Western counterparts in promoting use of domestic energy sources. The Asia-Pacific region holds 30 percent of the world's coal reserves, but only 6 percent of its gas and 4 percent of its oil. The possibility of expanding the use of coal is limited by environmental considerations. The further development of liquefied natural gas (LNG) and nuclear energy is hampered by very high capital costs.

Nor is it likely that Asia can substantially increase its energy efficiency, thereby reducing dependence on oil. Throughout most of Asia, oil intensity, or the amount of oil needed per unit of GDP growth, is relatively high. Although oil intensity has been falling everywhere, including Asia, it is still 2.5 times higher than in the OECD countries.

Towards A New Concept of Gulf Security

The West's exclusive military presence in the Gulf is generally resented in the region, and thus cannot provide security indefinitely. A new, balanced system of Gulf security is required, one which involves all of the countries of the Gulf as well as those outside it that have vital interests in the region. As this study has shown, Asia-Pacific countries have a large and growing stake in the stability of the Gulf. Asian countries must therefore achieve a level of involvement in the security of the Gulf that is commensurate with the region's importance as a source of energy supplies. China, Japan, and possibly India should share the burden, military and otherwise, of ensuring stability in the Gulf. However, these contributions must be accompanied, if not preceded by, efforts by Gulf countries themselves to reach a *modus vivendi* with each other. Towards that end, the countries bordering the Gulf should enter into non-aggression pacts, guaranteed by the United States and the United Kingdom, and supported both by other members of the UN Security Council and by major Asian powers such as Japan and India.

Energy Ties and "Policy Gaps"

John Mitchell

The energy relationships between Gulf oil producing and Asia-Pacific oil consuming countries are evolving in the context of profound global changes. The end of the Cold War, the communications revolution, and the retreat of the state from its leading role in the economy are just some of the developments that are transforming geopolitics and business everywhere, including Asia. The world energy market is not functioning independently of these changes, but rather is adapting as well as contributing to them.

New technologies, along with changes in energy policies, have yielded a steady increase in oil production outside OPEC and the former Soviet Union.[1] Over the period 1965-96, oil production for the "rest of the world" was the most predictable, stable variable. [See Graph 1.] Many official forecasters did not expect this. In fact, they had predicted that the rest of the world would quickly follow the US example of declining production from mature fields. Energy policies for the past two decades have tended to reflect this thinking. They have been based on the assumption that so-called "dependence on OPEC" would grow and that, consequently, the world might face energy-related problems reminiscent of the 1970s. Yet, these expectations have proved to be wrong, and current trends suggest a different future.

The Oil Outlook
1. Production Outside the Middle East
Non-OPEC oil production might eventually decline, but there is no sign that this will occur in the foreseeable future. Since oil prices have fallen below $20 per barrel, companies have invested in expanding production of Canadian heavy oil and in converting Venezuelan extra heavy oil to light components. Both of these resources have large potential reserves. Oil production growth in Russia and other countries of the former Soviet Union (FSU) is expected to resume. In future, these producers can be added to the non-OPEC category, given that, within a free market framework, their energy industries will tend to behave like

Graph 1
Oil Production* 1965-96

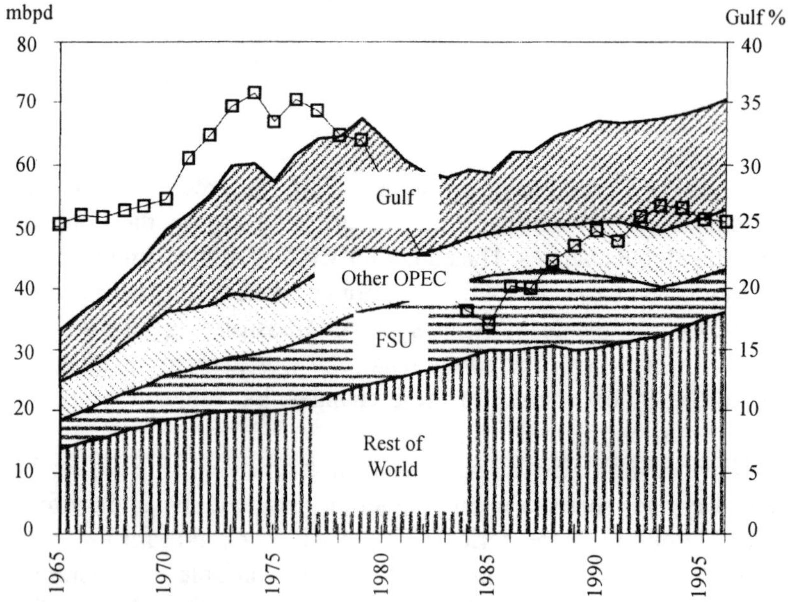

* In millions of barrels per day (mbpd)
Source: *BP Statistical Review* (London: British Petroleum, 1997).

others in this group.

Graph 2 depicts global energy production to the year 2020, and assumes that oil production from the "rest of the world" will grow at its historic annual rate of about 600,000 barrels per day (b/d).[2] Under this scenario, oil supply disruptions similar to those that contributed to the price shocks of 1973 and 1979-80 might occur. Competition between producers will continue, reducing the likelihood that an aggressive producers' oil price cartel will emerge. Yet, over the next five years, unlike in the 1980s, there will be relatively small spare production capacity.

Oil price behavior will resemble that of other commodities: prices will rise and fall according to mismatches between supply capacity and demand. The 1990 and 1996 price surges, which each lasted for about one year, suggest that upward price shocks are likely to be short-term phenomena. However, the downward price shocks of 1986 and 1998 were of a different character. "Overproduction" in the years leading up to these crises, which caused surpluses, was the primary reason for plummeting oil prices. To counteract this, major producers (e.g., Saudi Arabia) in 1986 and a wide group of producers in 1998 took defensive

Graph 2
Oil Production* 1995-2020

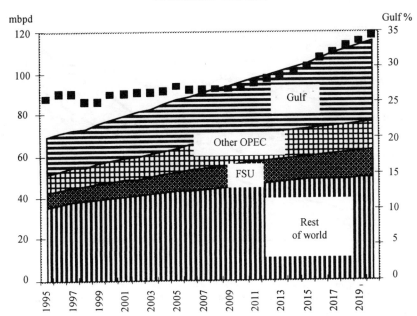

* In millions of barrels per day (mbpd)
Source: *BP Statistical Review* (London: British Petroleum, 1997).

action. The risk of steeply falling prices has not disappeared. Producers in the Middle East and outside the region have the reserve capacity to support much higher levels of production. The engine of competition will keep pumping.

2. The Geopolitical Basis of Competition in the Middle East

The governments of Middle East oil exporting countries have similar revenue objectives. They must meet the social needs of rapidly growing populations, fulfill the requirements for national defense in an unstable, highly militarized regional environment, and exercise influence beyond their borders partly in order to legitimize their rule.

Yet, Middle East oil producers have different current and future capacities to meet these objectives. They differ in terms of the ratio between their populations and their oil production capacities. They also differ in terms of the ratio between their current production capacities and potential reserves. It is therefore virtually impossible to design a "fair" allocation of oil revenue. Different price levels imply different levels of demand for Middle East oil and different shares of that demand. At low prices, Saudi Arabia and Iraq can increase volumes proportionately more

Graph 3
Energy Consumption 1965-96

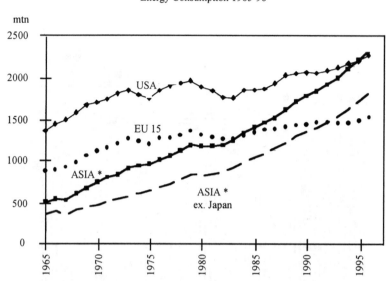

* In millions of tons (mtn)
Source: *BP Statistical Review* (London: British Petroleum, 1997).   * Asia excludes FSU

than Iran and the UAE. At high prices, Saudi Arabia faces the danger of being left as the residual supplier. Thus, in the coming years, as in recent times, Middle East producers might have to compete with each another for "sharing by shocks." The overall effect of this competition, which is good news for importers, will be to maintain long run pressure to expand production.

3. Policy Implications for Importers

In the long run, the growth of non-OPEC oil production, coupled with competition between countries that have large oil reserves, will secure the growth of supply. Policies and institutions that encourage these developments globally will provide importers with structural security. Reducing oil imports is not the only way for importers to avoid oil dependence. In fact, experience has shown that this approach is, as often as not, both costly and unnecessary. Instead, importers should aim for global expansion of competing oil supplies and national "self-sufficiency" alternatives.

Asia's Role in the World Oil Market

1. Asian Dimensions and Perspectives

Asia is an increasingly important part of the global energy market.

Graph 4
Oil Growth* from 1986

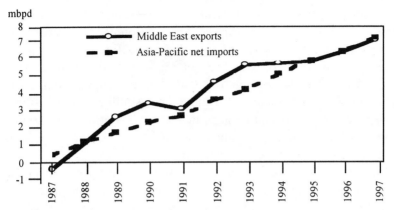

* In millions of barrels per day (mbpd)
Source: *BP Statistical Review* (London: British Petroleum, 1997).

Economic expansion in China, the Asia-Pacific region, and South Asia has generated some of the highest energy demand growth rates. In fact, in recent years, Asian energy consumption has eclipsed that of other geographic areas. By 1996, Asian energy consumption had exceeded that of the United States and, excluding Japan's consumption, had surpassed that of the European Union. [See Graph 3.]

Clearly, then, Asia matters more to the world energy market than it did 20 years ago, when the traditional energy policies of the OECD were formed. Then, the geopolitics of energy revolved primarily around the OECD, OPEC, the United States, and the Middle East. Now, the energy policies of the Asian countries affect the world balance. Asian choices about nuclear electricity, gas pipelines, and the use of coal affect the world fuel mix, the degree of competition in the petroleum market, and the risk of climate change.

In the oil sector, there is a high degree of interdependence between Middle East producers and Asian importers. Over the period 1986-97, the rise in Middle East production was closely correlated with the growth in oil consumption in the Asia Pacific region. [See Graph 4.] Clearly, Asian markets are very important to Middle East oil exporters. About 60 percent of Middle East oil exports are sold to the rest of Asia, while only 40 percent are sold to the rest of the world.

Middle East exporters have individual and collective interests in developing their positions in the Asian energy market. There are things that these exporters can do to secure their individual market shares, while reassuring importers that are concerned about security of supply. One path they can follow is to invest downstream. There have been some attempts to do so, mainly by Saudi Arabia. In fact, Saudi Aramco's strategic objective is to channel at least half its oil exports through its own refineries. However, Saudi Aramco has encountered obstacles in pursuing this goal. The scope for building new refineries in Europe is limited, and existing facilities are not profitable. Meanwhile, Saudi Aramco has succeeded in acquiring only limited refining interests in South Korea, the Philippines and India, and is still negotiating these arrangements in China and perhaps in Japan. Kuwait has a stake in a refinery in India, while the Iranian National Oil Company (INOC) is involved in a refinery project in Pakistan.

It is possible that recent events in importing countries may open the way to more investments. Yet, unfortunately, government policies in China, South Korea, India, Pakistan, and some other countries have not been conducive to foreign investment in downstream projects. The smaller markets that welcome foreign refiners (e.g., Singapore, Thailand, and the Philippines) are very competitive, and may be difficult to buy into at a good price.

2. The Effect of the "Asian Shocks"

Because the turmoil in Asia has not abated, its effects cannot yet be fully determined. Yet, it is clear that Asia is suffering from several types of crises. The first is a short-term financial crisis of the kind experienced by Thailand, South Korea, and Indonesia. The second is a macroeconomic crisis with a structural base, such as Japan faces. The third, exemplified by Indonesia, is a political crisis triggered by unpopular measures to deal with the financial crisis.

As of June 1998, the conventional wisdom among energy forecasters seemed to be that the worst surprises were over. By that time, they had already revised downward their earlier estimates of Asian energy demand. [See Chart 1.] Provisional figures[3] provided by the New York-based Energy Intelligence Group in May 1998 showed demand in India, Japan, Korea, and Thailand 430,000 b/d lower than in the previous year. In June 1998, the Paris-based International Energy Agency (IEA) reduced by 633,000 b/d its October 1997 forecast for demand growth in these countries.[4] The 1998 oil demand projections for Indonesia and Malaysia were 220,000 b/d lower than those made one year earlier.

Two crucial factors will determine the extent of the fall off in Asian energy demand: the rate of increase in Japan's oil demand and China's ability to sustain economic growth over the next two years. If, for the year

Chart 1
Oil Demand* Comparison of 1998 to 1997

	May 1998 vs May 1997	Forecast 1998 vs 1997
Japan, Korea, India, Thailand	-430	-630
Indonesia, Malaysia	n.a.	-220
China	+300	+250

* In millions of barrels per day (mbpd)
Source: *BP Statistical Review* (London: British Petroleum, 1997).

as a whole, Japanese oil demand does not fall and Chinese economic growth holds up, the Asian crises will have a limited effect on global oil demand. Japan alone accounts for one quarter of Asia's total oil consumption. South East Asia and South Korea together barely match this figure, while the balance of Asian oil consumption is made up of countries that have so far avoided a serious crisis.

A pessimistic view of the *medium term* effect of the 1998 Asian economic crises is that growth in Asian oil demand, taken as a whole, will stop for a period of three years and then resume at its previous rate. [See Graph 5.] If, over the next two-to-three years, there were no increase in oil demand in Asia as a whole, the growth in world demand would roughly match the growth in oil production from non-OPEC producers, including those of the former Soviet Union. Under these circumstances, OPEC producers could not expect any increase in demand for their oil, which would pose serious economic problems. In turn, these could lead to political problems, as recent experiences in some Asian countries show.

In the longer term, some studies estimate that demand will "bounce back." The Energy Information Agency (EIA) of the US Department of Energy, for example, projects higher rates of growth. According to these estimates, the level of demand by the year 2015 might be as great as that which had been forecast before the Asian financial crisis began.[5]

3. Coping with Supply Disruptions

For many countries that export oil, this resource is the main source of foreign exchange earnings and government revenue. In the case of Gulf producers, oil revenues enable governments to avoid taxing their citizens and to subsidize oil prices in the domestic economy. The population growth rates of these countries are high, as are the demands for social

Graph 5
Incremental Oil Demand*

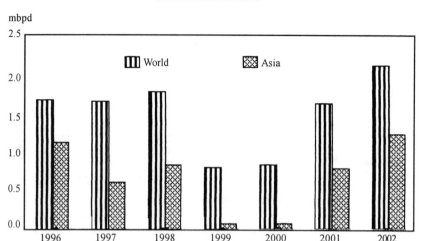

* In millions of barrels per day (mbpd)
Source: *BP Statistical Review* (London: British Petroleum, 1997).

services and employment. Under the pessimistic scenario for Asian oil demand growth described earlier, Middle East governments would face more severe financial constraints and possibly greater social and political pressures than they do now.

Although maintaining the flow of oil is in everyone's interest, it is of particular concern to Asian energy importers. Some Asian countries (including Japan, Korea, Thailand, Philippines, and Singapore) depend on imported oil for more than 50 percent of their total energy supplies. Disruptions to oil supplies will pose serious challenges for these importers. With the exception of Japan, which holds a high level of strategic stocks and is a full member of the International Energy Agency (IEA), these importers would have to resort to the spot market to cope with supply shortfalls. In turn, competitive bidding on the spot market would affect oil prices globally: oil security against price shocks cannot be achieved in isolation.

Since 1990, it has become obvious that political and military measures are the main protection for oil importers against supply disruptions. The coalition against Iraq in 1990 established a cold peace in the Middle East, at least for oil exporters. US military power was the key to that peace. Asian countries (e.g., Japan, Saudi Arabia, and Kuwait) contributed primarily to defray the financial cost of the UN military intervention against Iraq. The February 1998 Iraq crisis, however, might

Graph 6
Middle East Oil as % of 1996

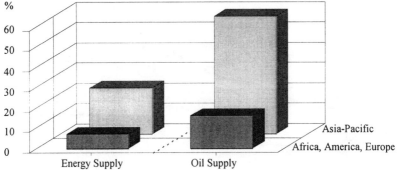

Source: *BP Statistical Review* (London: British Petroleum, 1997).

have marked the end of the Gulf War era. During this crisis, the United States was unable to reconstitute the international coalition to support military action. Nor were US officials able to negotiate a peaceful outcome without the diplomatic intervention of France and the personal diplomacy of UN Secretary General Kofi Annan.

Looking to the future, one must consider whether "Western" political and military interventions will provide effective protection for intra-Asia oil supplies in future disruption scenarios. Effectiveness will depend on effort, and effort will depend partly on the interest of the countries concerned. Asia as a whole has a large and growing stake in maintaining the flow of oil from the Middle East.

Oil from the Middle East represents 58 percent of oil consumption in the Asia-Pacific region and 23 percent of its energy. [See Graph 6.] The figures for Africa, America, and Europe combined are 16 percent and 7 percent respectively. In 1996, Middle East oil comprised 18 percent of US oil consumption and 4 percent of US energy consumption. Although these figures are not the only index of national and political interests, they must be part of the equation. Asian oil importing countries might not always be able to depend on Western political and military protection of their oil supplies when disruptions occur.

4. The Natural Gas Option

There is another contrast between Asia and the rest of the world, namely, its use of natural gas. Natural gas has many attractions as a fuel: low sulphur content, lower CO_2 emissions per unit of useful energy, and so on. Yet, except in those countries which produce natural gas, it is a smaller

Graph 7
Gas Share of Energy (%)

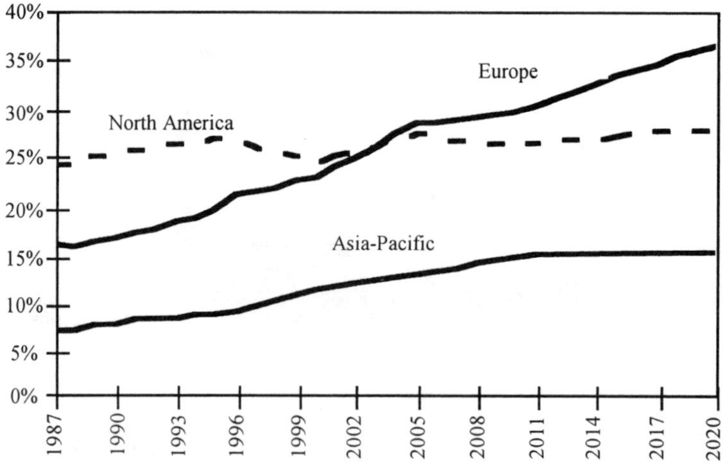

Source: *BP Statistical Review* (London: British Petroleum, 1997).

share of the fuel mix in Asia than it is in the rest of the world. [See Graph 7.] What, then, can explain the relatively small share of natural gas in Asia's energy mix?

EIA projections show the natural gas share of total energy growing more slowly in Asia than in Europe, and well below that of the United States or Europe. The European growth in the use of natural gas will be based on the development of long-distance imports, as that of Asia must be. Currently in Asia, the gas share of the fuel mix depends on whether it is available locally or not. Where gas is not available in the country, the gas share is even lower than the number shown.

The Asia-Pacific markets are the only practical ones for the very large gas reserves of Eastern Russia and the Middle East. The demand for gas exceeds the supply in China, as it does in East and South East Asia.[6] [See Chart 2.] Future gas growth in the Asia-Pacific region, as in Europe, will depend on developing long-distance gas imports. In turn, this will depend on developing transportation systems at a cost that leaves sufficient incentive for the producers after matching the price of competing fuels such as coal and fuel oil in the importing market.

The cost-effective construction of transportation systems to deliver natural gas to Asian markets is partly a question of politics. Cross-border pipelines are costly and complex projects which the governments concerned must agree either to build themselves or to provide conditions for private sector investment. It is also a question of cost containment.

Chart 2
Asian Gas Options* 2020 (bcm/year)

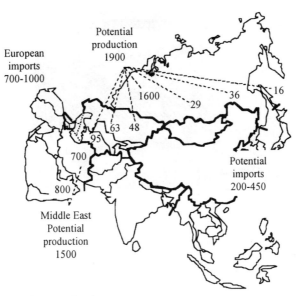

Potential
production
1900

European
imports
700-1000

1600   36   16

29

63   48

95

700

Potential
imports
200-450

800

Middle East
Potential
production
1500

* In billions of cubic meters (bcm)
Source: *BP Statistical Review* (London: British Petroleum, 1997).

The pipelines will have local construction costs in local currency. Cooperation between contractors and developers, such as occurred in the North Sea oil projects, might be necessary to reduce costs.

The position of China is critical. It is the nearest market to the potential gas suppliers. China has recently reached agreement on gas development projects with Russia and Kazakhstan. The current political climate seems more conducive to progress on these projects than does the commercial environment. Nevertheless, if China's plans for two major pipelines within the country are realized, the result could be gas deliveries to China equivalent to about 2 million barrels per day by the year 2020. Although this would constitute a relatively small fraction of world energy supplies, it would represent a large portion of China's potential energy import requirements and therefore affect international oil markets.

5. The Nuclear Option

Asian countries presently hold about 15 percent of the world's nuclear generating capacity, concentrated mainly in Japan and South Korea. Iran, Taiwan, North Korea, India, and Pakistan also plan to develop nuclear generating capacity. This will boost Asia's share of world capacity to over 20 percent by the year 2010. In contrast, none of the countries of

Chart 3
Nuclear Capacity*

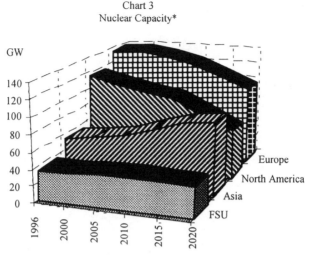

* In gigawatts (GW)
Source: *BP Statistical Review* (London: British Petroleum, 1997).

Europe or North America plans a substantial increase in nuclear generating capacity. [See Chart 3.] In fact, according to the EIA reference projection, world nuclear capacity has already stopped growing, and will fall about 15 percent by the year 2020. In North America and Europe, the decline will be about 50 percent and 30 percent, respectively.

There are, of course, elements of uncertainty in these forecasts. The lives of existing plants are being extended. Higher operating efficiencies are being achieved. There is a powerful economic incentive to keep nuclear plants running because of the very high costs of decommissioning them. Some of the plans by Asian countries (and others) to expand nuclear generating capacity might not be fulfilled. Nevertheless, these projections clearly indicate that different parts of the world have dramatically different views about the acceptability and economics of nuclear energy; that the center of gravity of the nuclear construction industry will shift to Asia, leaving the US and European-based companies without any home market; and that the problem of storage, transport and processing of nuclear waste will continue to grow because of Asian decisions. The connection between nuclear fuels, nuclear waste, and nuclear weapons will continue to be an international issue. Asian countries will be involved and their voices will be important in addressing this issue.

Finally, were Asia and the rest of the world eventually to see the nuclear problem in the same way, the effect on the market for fossil fuels could be quite large: if Asian countries follow the US and European examples, Asia will cease to expand nuclear capacity and will look for alternative fuels. In Europe and North America, the only factor likely to revive nuclear growth would be the realization that the cost of mitigating carbon dioxide emissions by any other means were unacceptable. In the first case, the demand for fossil fuels would expand, while in the second, it would contract.

Narrowing the "Policy Gap"

Although many features of the Asian energy outlook are different from those of the rest of the world, there is little debate about Asian issues in the energy geopolitical arena. There is no appropriate Asian institution spanning exporters, importers, and all the relevant industries.

Furthermore, an agenda for such a debate might include defining conditions for reducing the risk of investing in cross-border energy supplies: developing new oil and gas production capacity, building new gas transportation systems (pipeline or LNG), and managing nuclear operating and waste management risks. It might also include developing agreed strategies for mitigating the effects of disruptions, such as establishing strategic oil stocks in importing countries which are not IEA members, and investing in financial and commercial instruments to ease balance of payment problems associated with oil price shocks. Finally, this agenda might include promoting the security of market outlets.

The European Union (EU), the North American Free Trade Agreement (NAFTA), the Free Trade Area of the Americas (FTAA), and the Energy Charter Treaty all contain elements of a regional approach to energy problems within their respective institutional settings. It might be valuable for key Asian countries to explore the possibilities for a regional approach to Asia's energy challenges that is compatible with their multilateral obligations and the continued development of the global trading and investment system.

Notes

[1] There have been technological advances in combined cycle gas turbine generating and seismic exploration capacity; in the control of deviated drilling and the completion and operation of subsea wells; and in cathodic protection for pipes and tanks. Meanwhile, governments have promoted competition in, and in many cases have privatized, the electricity industry, paving the way for new producers to apply combined cycle gas technology. They have also instituted more rational upstream tax

regimes, and have opened up new acreage to competing investors under production sharing and similar contracts.

[2] Although the oil demand figures in this graph are based on the reference case of the US Energy Information Agency's (EIA) *1998 International Energy Outlook*, the figures for oil production growth "for the rest of the world" differ from those of the EIA study. See US Energy Information Administration, *1998 International Energy Outlook* (Washington, DC: Government Printing Office, 1998).

[3] *Oil Market Intelligence*, 6 June 1998.

[4] International Energy Agency, *Monthly Oil Market Report*, 6 June 1998.

[5] Energy Information Agency, *1998 International Energy Outlook* (Washington, DC: Government Printing Office, 1998).

[6] The potential supply figures are indicative only. They are the result of dividing the proved reserve numbers in each area by 30. In real life, developments would be smaller and reserves would be larger.

Energy and Geopolitics:
Asian Perspectives

China's Stabilizing Role

Yang Guang

A lthough oil is not China's leading primary energy source, it is nonetheless an increasingly important part of the country's energy mix. In recent years, however, the growth of China's oil demand has exceeded the expansion of its domestic oil production. This imbalance has resulted in a continuous erosion of China's oil exporting capacity. It has also transformed China from a net exporter to a net importer of oil products. In turn, this has expanded China's interests in the Gulf and interactions with Gulf countries.

A New Reality: China as a Net Oil Importer

The critical developments in China's energy profile mentioned above stem from changes on both the demand and the supply sides— changes which seem irreversible, at least until early in the next century. On the demand side, rapid and sustained economic growth is the most important factor that has driven and will continue to drive, high energy demand. From 1990 to 1995, for example, China's average annual GDP growth rate was 12 percent. The elasticity coefficient of energy consumption shows that every one percent increase in GDP led to a 0.528 percent increase in oil consumption.

The impact of economic growth on oil and oil product consumption in China can be understood in terms of several specific causal factors. The first is the Chinese economy's structure of production during the "take-off" stage. In this period, energy-intensive industries (e.g., chemical, petrochemical, metallurgical and building materials) have played an essential role in China's industrialization. This is unlikely to change in the short term.

The second is the development of the transportation sector. In developed countries, this sector is normally the leading consumer of petroleum products. In China, the transportation sector has developed rapidly. From the early 1980s to the mid-1990s, for example, the number of vehicles for civilian use in China increased by 4.6 times, while the consumption of petroleum products for transportation quadrupled. This trend too will continue.

The third is China's low per capita energy consumption, equivalent to 664 kilograms in 1994. This lags far behind the average per capita energy consumption of both developed and developing countries. However, in light of China's rapid economic growth and the improvement in the standard of living of its population, there is tremendous potential for the growth of energy consumption and the possible conversion of this potential into real demand.

The fourth is that the country's economic take-off and the growth of per capita income are conducive to a structural change in energy consumption in favor of energies of quality and high efficiency such as oil, natural gas, and electricity at the expense of coal and biological energies. This has proved to be the case in many developed economies as well as in the Asian "tiger" economies, and is presently taking place in China. This tendency is especially evident in the southeast coastal provinces, which have experienced the most rapid economic growth. That is why, during the first half of the 1990s, the elasticity coefficient of oil consumption (0.528) was higher than that of national energy consumption (0.458).

Environmental concerns have reinforced the tendency in favor of greater reliance on oil and natural gas. Statistics indicate that burning coal, which accounts for 75 percent of China's primary energy consumption, is responsible for 85 percent of SO_2, 70 percent of smoke and dust as well as 85 percent of CO_2 emissions. Therefore, in order to achieve sustainable development, the development of coal energy has to be brought under control. It is predicted that, between the years 1995 and 2010, coal's share in China's primary energy consumption structure will fall from 75.5 to 64 percent, while oil's share will rise from 17.3 to 19.4 percent.[1] Although natural gas, hydro-electricity and nuclear power will also expand their shares, they will remain marginal elements of China's primary energy mix.

The fifth factor driving high energy demand, especially demand for oil, is China's relatively low energy efficiency. This will continue to be the case until further progress is made in introducing and developing relevant technologies, and in rationalizing energy prices.

On the supply side, China's oil industry is in a period of transition. The Eastern oil fields were put into production between the 1950s and 1970s. Whereas these fields still account for the lion's share of Chinese oil production, they are expected to be replaced gradually by the newly discovered Western oil fields. Presently, however, production in the East has levelled off, while that in the West will require more time to develop.

Contrasting with the record-high increase in oil demand, the growth rate of oil production has plunged to an all-time low. Between 1990 and 1995, oil consumption grew at an average annual rate of 6.34 percent, while oil production rose at an average annual rate of just 1.64 percent.

The gap between domestic oil demand and supply is widening. It is predicted that, by the year 2010, China's oil demand will reach 280 million tons, of which only 180 million tons is expected to come from domestic sources. The net oil import of crude oil and oil products will increase from 34.3 million tons in 1997 to 100 million tons. In other words, by the year 2010, 35.7 percent of oil consumed by China will have to be imported.[2] However, the extent of China's oil import dependence should not be exaggerated. Various projections show that, although China's oil imports will be higher both in volume and as a proportion of world oil trade movements, they will represent only 2.3 percent of world oil production. This is minuscule compared to the net oil import volumes of the United States and Japan. In 1997, the United States imported 442.7 million tons of oil, while Japan imported 277.5 million tons. This was the equivalent of 12.7 percent and 8 percent, respectively, of world production that year—several times larger than that of China.[3]

A Paradox: Diversification Versus Concentration

Chinese officials have addressed the challenges posed by rapidly rising oil demand and oil import dependence in a variety of ways. They have instituted measures to conserve energy, to increase energy efficiency, and to intensify domestic oil and gas exploration. In order to expand domestic oil and gas production, they have opened exploration and development to foreign investors. In addition, they have sought to diversify China's international sources of oil supply.

China's efforts to diversify its international sources of oil supply have proved to be very successful. In 1990, 81.5 percent of China's oil imports had come from just three countries. At that time, Indonesia was the only country to supply China with more than one million tons of oil. Yet, in 1997, the number of countries supplying more than two million tons of oil to China increased to six: Oman (9.03 MT), Indonesia (6.59 MT), Yemen (4.06 MT), Angola (3.84 MT), Iran (2.76 MT) and Vietnam (1.42 MT). Meanwhile, Congo, Gabon, Saudi Arabia, Australia, Papua New Guinea, Egypt and Malaysia also emerged as sources of oil supply for China.[4]

As part of the diversification strategy, Chinese oil companies began to conduct transnational operations in 1993. So far, they have engaged in oil exploration and development projects in many countries, including the United States, Canada, Peru, Sudan, Papua New Guinea, and Venezuela.

Notwithstanding the progress made in diversifying its foreign sources of oil supplies, China has become more dependent on the Gulf countries. During the 1990s, the volume of China's oil imports from the Gulf region have grown at an average annual rate of 46.7 percent, exceeding the 42.8 percent average growth rate of total oil imports. Over the same period, China's total oil imports have increased in volume from 1.15 million tons to 16.78 million tons. In 1997, with the exception of Bahrain, all of the Gulf countries supplied oil to China.

Gulf oil-exporting countries possess two-thirds of the world's proven oil reserves. For this reason, the Gulf will occupy an even more significant place in the international oil market than it currently does. From the perspective of Gulf producers, China is a major potential customer. Gulf countries have factored this into their long-term market share strategies. Consequently, China's oil ties with the Gulf states will probably continue to develop in the coming years.

Central Asia is another promising source of oil for China. Most energy analysts believe that this region, especially the Caspian Sea area, holds substantial oil reserves, though they disagree as to the exact volume. If the problems of capital investment and transportation can be resolved smoothly, Central Asia might become a key source of supply for the world market and possibly form part of the Gulf-Central Asia energy axis early in the next century. Geographic proximity constitutes an unique advantage for Sino-Central Asian cooperation in the oil sector. In 1997, a Chinese oil company won the bid for a major oil development project in Kazakhstan. This marked the beginning of Sino-Central Asia energy cooperation.

China's Stabilizing Role

China's growing dependence on oil from the Gulf and, in the future, probably from Central Asia as well, will lead Chinese officials to devote closer attention to issues affecting peace and stability in these regions. This is not only understandable, but unavoidable, given that all of the major oil crises that have occurred since the early

1970s have stemmed from regional political crises.

As the new century draws closer, peace and stability in the Gulf and Central Asia remain no less elusive. The Middle East as a whole is plagued by deep-rooted religious and ethnic problems. Since 1996, the peace process has stagnated. Issues left over by the 1991 Gulf War have yet to be resolved. Adding to this climate of political uncertainty are the dismal prospects for economic growth for the Gulf states and the social costs of structural adjustment for the other Middle Eastern countries. Similarly, Central Asia suffers from a number of problems, including ethnic and territorial disputes. The countries bordering the Caspian Sea differ on how to divide it and distribute its natural resources. They, along with others, disagree about oil and gas pipeline routes, and these differences thinly mask competing geopolitical interests. Thus, in Central Asia as well as in the Gulf, there are many sources and signs of tension.

Oil importing countries, not to mention the countries of the Gulf and Central Asia themselves, have a common interest in peacefully resolving disputes and in preventing new conflicts from erupting. The fact that China shares this interest is evident in its policies towards the Gulf and Central Asia. In fact, the underlying principles and objectives of China's policies towards these regions are consistent with those which guide its foreign relations generally.

China's policies towards the Gulf and Central Asia reflect its domestic priorities. Over the past two decades, China's highest domestic priority has been economic development. Accordingly, the primary objective of China's diplomacy has been to create and maintain a peaceful international environment so as to achieve its economic development goals. China's approach to peace and stability in the Gulf contrasts with that of some Western countries, which stress the projection of military force near or in the Gulf. China's approach is based on the "Five Principles of Peaceful Coexistence:" mutual respect for territorial integrity and sovereignty, mutual non-aggression, non-interference in one other's internal affairs, equality and mutual benefit, and peaceful coexistence. China has strictly adhered to these principles in formulating its policies towards the Gulf and Central Asia. It has applied these principles both in its bilateral dealings with the countries of these regions, and through its positions and influence as a permanent member of the United Nations Security Council.

Chinese officials believe that the resolution of major Middle Eastern problems requires broad international efforts and mechanisms. Furthermore, they believe that these efforts and mechanisms must be inclusive; that is, developed not only with the involvement of outside players, but also with the agreement and participation of the countries of the region. Reflecting this belief, China's role in the pursuit of peace and stability mainly in the framework of UN initiatives and international treaties.

On the Arab-Israeli issue, China considers a political settlement to be the only way to end the conflict, and supports the "land for peace" approach. In addition using its vote in the UN Security Council to uphold justice and promote the peace process, China has taken advantage of its relationships of mutual trust with the countries concerned to encourage progress towards a political settlement. The establishment of official diplomatic ties with Israel in 1992 enabled China to play a more balanced and constructive role in this regard. China has opposed terrorism of all kinds. China has actively participated in UN peacekeeping efforts in the region by sending military observers to UNTSO, UNICOM and MINURSO.

With respect to Gulf security, China has worked with the other members of the Security Council. With China's cooperation, the Security Council adopted UN Resolution 598, which led to the 1987 cease-fire in the Iran-Iraq war. China condemned the invasion of Kuwait and, while not favoring the use of force against Iraq, has, since the Gulf War, consistently urged Iraq to comply fully with all of the relevant UN Security Council resolutions.

Arms control is an important and sensitive issue for the stability of the region. China's position on arms control is cautious, clear and responsible. In 1984, China signed the Convention on the Prohibition of the Development, Production, Stockpiling of Bacteriological (Biological) and Toxic Weapons and on Their Destruction (BWC); and, in 1993, signed the Convention on the Prohibition of the Development, Production, Stockpiling, and Use of Chemicals Weapons and on Their Destruction (CWC). As a signatory to these conventions, China has stood for the complete destruction and prohibition of these weapons not only in the Middle East, but throughout the world. China has worked towards the same objective with respect to nuclear weapons since acceding to the Treaty on the Non-Proliferation of Nuclear Weapons (NPT) in 1992. Regarding nuclear exports, China has pursued a policy of not supporting, encouraging or engaging in the proliferation of nuclear weapons. In May 1996, China pledged to refrain from furnishing nuclear assistance—

including exports of nuclear materials, personnel, exchange of technology, and other forms of cooperation—to countries which had not accepted International Atomic Energy Agency (IAEA) safeguards. In May 1997, the Chinese government published the Circular on Questions Pertaining to the Strict Implementation of China's Nuclear Exports Policy, which explicitly stipulates that no nuclear materials, facilities or related technologies exported by China may be supplied to or used by nuclear facilities which have not accepted IAEA safeguards. On June 10, 1998, China promulgated the Regulations on the Control of the Export of Dual-Use Nuclear Materials and Related Technology, thereby imposing strict control on the export of these items. China has supported the idea of making the Middle East not only a "nuclear-free," but a "weapons of mass destruction-free" zone.

Although the Middle East is considered the world's largest weapons market for conventional military equipment, China's involvement in this market is very limited in comparison with the leading exporters of military hardware such as the United States, France and Great Britain. Actually, China's export of military products did not start until the mid-1980s, and its total annual export value has not exceeded $1 billion since the late 1980s.[5] China is also very cautious and responsible regarding the transfer of missiles to the region. In fact, in 1992, China pledged to observe the guidelines and parameters of the Missile Technology Control Regime (MTCR).

Peace and stability in the surrounding countries is one of China's most important strategic objectives. In order to achieve this objective, China has promoted a new concept of security based on the notions of "mutual and equal security" and "seeking security by building mutual trust and dialogue." China has applied this concept to Central Asia, and has made concrete and substantial progress in its relationships with the countries of this region. Between 1994 and 1998, negotiations led to the signing of several treaties. The border issue between China and Kazakhstan has basically been settled. In April 1996, China, Russia, Kazakhstan, Kyrgyzstan, and Tajikistan signed the Agreement on Confidence-Building in the Military Field Along the Border Areas. The five signatories pledged that forces deployed in the border areas would not be used to attack each other. They also pledged to refrain from staging military exercises directed at one another, and to notify and invite one another to observe troop exercises. In April 1997, these same five states signed the Agreement on Mutual Reduction of Forces in the Border Areas, which stipulates that they shall reduce their forces in these areas to the minimum level compatible with their friendly and good-neighborly relations, a level that shall not exceed their defense needs. There is no doubt that the resolution of border issues between China and these neighbors has contributed to peace and stability in Central Asia, and will continue to do so.

Conclusion

China has become a net oil importer. This recent development has spurred closer energy ties between China and the Gulf states, and will probably foster similar ties between China and Central Asia in the not too distant future. However, instead of changing the basic objectives and principles of Chinese diplomacy, this new reality has provided an additional reason for China to adhere to them. China will thus continue to play the role of stabilizer in the Middle East and Central Asia.

Notes

[1] *China's Energy Development Report* (Beijing: Economic Management Publishing House, 1997).

[2] Ibid.

[3] Ibid.

[4] Ibid.

[5] *Journal of International Petroleum Economics*, No. 3, 1998.

Indo-Gulf Relations: Dimensions of Security*

Sujit Dutta

India's increasing energy consumption, and the corresponding rise in its dependence on oil imports from the Gulf, is a major driving force of expanding Gulf-Asia energy ties. The development of closer energy ties between the two regions, specifically between India and the Gulf countries, raises several important questions. How will India's more extensive penetration of the Gulf energy market affect the security of that region? In turn, how will India's reliance on the Gulf to meet its growing energy requirements influence both its energy and security policies? Furthermore, what considerations will guide Indian policymakers in formulating these policies? This study will explore these questions by discussing India's energy consumption patterns, examining its current energy security policies, and exploring the military and non-military dimensions of Indo-Gulf relations.

India's Energy Requirements

Numerous studies have shown that Asia is on its way to becoming the primary market for Gulf, and possibly Central Asian, oil and gas. These same studies have indicated that India and China are the principal driving forces of growing energy consumption in the Asia-Pacific region. This is primarily because both India and China have large populations and expanding energy-intensive industrial bases.

India's energy consumption rate has already changed. Though still relatively low, this rate is rising. In fact, in the coming years, there is a distinct possibility that India's energy consumption will grow rapidly, if not exponentially. India's energy demand is expected to increase at an annual rate of 4.625 percent through the year 2010.

India's current primary energy mix is diversified, though unbalanced. Coal fulfills 60 percent of India's primary energy needs. Oil, though a far smaller fraction, nonetheless forms 18.6 percent share of India's energy requirements. India's demand for oil, moreover, is rising

* This text is an edited version of the contributor's remarks made at the Middle East Institute's conference on "Gulf-Asia Energy Security" held at the Madison Hotel, Washington, DC, 9 July 1998.

at an average annual rate of 10 percent. Hydropower (8.9 percent), natural gas (8.2 percent) and nuclear power (2 percent) complete India's current energy profile. This is likely to change only marginally before the year 2010. In the intervening time, modest increases are expected in the shares of hydropower and gas in India's overall energy mix. Meanwhile, nuclear power is expected to stagnate at 1.5-2 percent.

Energy Supply Security

India's past experiences guide its current energy policy. The first experience was the 1973-74 oil price rise and the instability in the oil market that it caused. This oil "shock" had a major adverse impact on India primarily because of the importance of oil in the country's overall trade structure. This has not changed. Even at current low prices, the value of India's annual oil imports exceeds $10 billion. The second experience was Iraq's invasion of Kuwait and the subsequent Gulf War. Besides disrupting oil supplies, these conflicts destroyed infrastructure and other assets in which India had interests. The lessons of these experiences are apparent in India's current energy strategy.

The overall aim of India's energy strategy is stable oil supplies at relatively low prices. India's energy strategy seeks to diversify both its domestic and foreign sources of energy supplies. In the case of oil, India has long relied on the Gulf as its main source of supply. Currently, India imports about 35 million tons of oil annually. The bulk of this comes from four countries: Saudi Arabia, Kuwait, UAE, and Iran. Prior to the Gulf War, Iraq too had served as a major source of oil. In fact, Indo-Iraq relations were extensive both in the industrial and energy supply areas. The UN-mandated sanctions against Iraq have resulted in the suspension of these activities. Meanwhile, the volume of oil supplies from the former Soviet Union has sharply declined.

India has devoted considerable effort to diversify its sources of oil as well as to find alternative sources of natural gas. India has sought, for example, to develop gas supplies from Bangladesh and Myanmar in the East. It has opened up large tracts of off shore oil and gas exploration with multinational corporations in the South and West. India has also pursued new sources of energy supplies, particularly of gas, from Iran, Oman and Turkmenistan. The Indian oil industry is actively involved in Kazakhstan, Azerbaijan, Iran, and Oman both in oil and gas exploration and in downstream projects. An additional component of India's energy diversification strategy—spurred by its unstable relationship with Pakistan and by turmoil in Afghanistan—is the development of an Indo-

Iranian railway system as a secondary energy supply corridor. Notwithstanding the success of these efforts, the Gulf is still the primary source of India's oil imports, and will continue to be.

Military Aspects of Security

Unsurprisingly, India's oil dependence on the Gulf has a direct bearing on the country's military planning and preparations. The Indian navy and air force are critically important in terms of protecting supply lanes. Accordingly, India is engaged in ongoing efforts to strengthen the armed forces to perform this mission.

Over the years, India has developed a set of military relationships with Saudi Arabia, Iran, Qatar, Oman, and (prior to the Gulf War) Iraq. India has had two primary motivations for pursuing military ties with Gulf countries: to support the overall development of its bilateral relationships and to promote regional security. These military ties have taken the form of joint military exercises and exchanges, as well as confidence-building measures. It is important to emphasize, however, that they have *not* included conventional arms transfers from India to the Gulf countries. Although at one time Iran had expressed an interest in purchasing weapons, Indian authorities declined to sell them. Nor has India provided nuclear technology or other related assistance to any of the countries of the region.

It is possible that weapons transfers might eventually become a component of Indo-Gulf relations, as Gulf-Asia energy ties intensify and as India's own energy dependence on the region increases. Nevertheless, the prevailing view in India is that Indo-Gulf military ties should seek to foster, and might some day evolve into, cooperative mechanisms within a broader multilateral regional security structure.

Social, Religious and Political Aspects of Security

India's relations with the Gulf countries have an important social dimension. Over the past 15-20 years, the size of the Indian expatriate community residing in the Gulf has risen dramatically. There are currently about 2.5 to 3 million Indian workers, technicians and managers in the Gulf region. This expatriate work force was hit hard by the Gulf War, which resulted in lost jobs, property and remittances. When war broke out, the Government of India mounted a large-scale operation to evacuate them. Since that time, Indian officials have remained concerned about the safety of the Indian expatriate community in the Gulf.

India and the Gulf are also linked at the societal level by religion.

India has the second-largest Muslim population in the world, about 130 million people. Although most Indian Muslims are Sunni, there are a significant number of Shi'a Muslims in India as well. This encourages Indian authorities to develop friendly and constructive relations with Gulf countries. Furthermore, because Sunni-Shi'a differences to some extent shape the politics of the Muslim world—at the national and interstate levels—Indian policymakers recognize the need to follow a strategy towards Muslim countries that accommodates these differences. In terms of the Gulf, this means that India must maintain a balance between friendly relations with Iran and fruitful relations with the Arab states.

The religious-political linkages between India and the Gulf are important for yet another reason. Iran, Saudi Arabia and others have been actively involved, both in religious and political terms, with Muslim groups in India. This interest and involvement is most apparent with regard to Hindu nationalist issues. The Organization of the Islamic Conference (OIC), of which the Gulf countries are members, has been long been an active and interested party on the Kashmir issue. Meanwhile, given the fabric of its own society, India favors the development of secular, democratic trends in the Gulf region and elsewhere in the Muslim world. Therefore, on the political and religious side, there is a constant need for dialogue between India and the Gulf states.

Conclusion

India has a strong interest in the peace and stability of the Gulf region. Yet, it does not appear that the current security problems of the Gulf will be quickly and easily overcome. Furthermore, it is not likely that the United States will abandon its role, or be replaced, as the guarantor of Gulf security any time soon. Nevertheless, US military paramountcy in the Gulf is not necessarily a permanent feature of the Gulf security environment, nor is it necessarily the ideal approach to lasting peace and stability in the region.

In the current circumstances, from an Indian perspective, an improvement in US-Iranian relations would be beneficial for the region and would serve India's interests. It would facilitate the flow of investments into the region's energy sector. Perhaps more importantly, it would permit the design of a new framework for regional security. India favors the development of creative and cooperative approaches to Gulf security. In fact, through the power of example and experience, India and

East Asia might be helpful in devising innovative approaches to Gulf security.The Asian Regional Forum, for instance, has brought together ASEAN members, other East Asian countries, India, the United States, and Australia in order to explore the overall management of security. This is still at the level of discussion, rather than at the level of a collective security framework. Nevertheless, a structure like this one, emerging alongside a revitalized and possibly expanded Gulf Cooperation Council (GCC) and an APEC-like institution, could serve as a mechanism to make the transition from a US-dominated to a multilateral structure of security.

Energy Market Forces and Power Politics

Katsuhiko Suetsugu

The Asian financial crisis and economic recession have slowed the development of Gulf-Asia energy relations, but have not put an end to them. This is an opportune time to assess the extent of the damage inflicted by Asia's ailing economies on Gulf-Asia energy ties and their prospects for recovery. It is also an opportune time to explore the energy relationships that exist between these two regions in terms of their political and geopolitical significance.

The Asian Economic Crisis and the Middle East

Between 1980 and 1995, Asia's average oil consumption growth rate was 5.6 percent. The Asian currency crisis and economic recession, however, have significantly reduced oil demand in the region. Asia's average oil consumption growth rates are 2.5 percent lower than they were during the first half of 1997 and 2.8 percent lower than in the first six months of 1998. This is a sharp fall off from the January-June 1996 growth rate of 5.6 percent. Yet, Asian oil consumption is expected to increase at an annual rate of between 2.5 percent to 3.5 percent through the year 2001. If this projection proves correct, Asian countries' oil consumption growth rates will exceed the 2 percent growth estimated for the world.

The situation in South Korea exemplifies what is happening elsewhere in Asia. According to the Korea Petroleum Association, South Korea's domestic consumption of petroleum products decreased by 16.4 percent in January-April 1998, compared to the same period in 1997 due to the currency crisis and economic recession. (In Thailand and Indonesia, consumption decreased by 4.2 percent and 1.3 percent, respectively, while Japan's consumption increased by just 1.2 percent). Korean imports of crude oil and petroleum products fell by 10 percent, the largest decline since the oil crisis of the 1970s. South Korea's exports of petroleum products averaged 830,000 b/d during the period January-April 1998, an increase of 34.8 percent over the same period last year. According to some reports, South Korea has partially drawn down its petroleum stockpiles in order to preserve foreign exchange reserves and rescue domestic oil companies.

Asian countries' dependence on petroleum from the Middle East has slowed slightly because of the economic recession; however, their dependency is nonetheless expected to remain at a high level. Since Asia's currency crisis and economic recession began in July 1997, Asian currencies—excluding the Japanese yen—have depreciated by approximately 60 to 70 percent. This has caused the relative price of oil for these countries to rise. Urgently yet reluctantly, Asian countries have increased the price of domestic petroleum products, and have cut fuel subsidies in accordance with IMF recommendations. In Thailand, plans for petroleum complexes have been abandoned, while in Korea a major oil refiner has faced a corporate financial crisis. In Japan, the excessive supply of oil in the world market has kept the domestic price of gasoline low despite the increased refining costs stemming from the depreciation of the yen against the US dollar.

As a result of the IMF financial bailout, South Korea's foreign currency situation has improved, while its oil imports have been consistently maintained. Yet, oil suppliers such as Saudi Aramco have imposed strict payment conditions upon South Korean as well as Japanese petroleum companies.

Although the prospects for the recovery of Asian oil demand are, of course, uncertain, many studies have been released on this subject. The East-West Center of the University of Hawaii, for example, provides petroleum product demand forecasts for Asia based on two scenarios. Under the "moderate recovery" scenario, the average annual growth rate of Asian oil demand is projected to be 3.6 percent for the period 1997-2000, 3.7 percent for the period 2000-2005, and 3.3 percent for the period 2000-2010. Under the "slow recovery" scenario, total regional oil demand is expected to increase at an average annual rate of 2.5 percent between 1997 and the year 2000. The regional petroleum demand forecast up to the year 2010 under the slow recovery scenario is 1.2 million b/d lower than under the moderate recovery scenario.

Asian Oil Import Dependence on the Middle East

Asian oil dependence on the Middle East is not a transitory phenomenon. A key reason for this dependence is that Asian demand for oil is primarily for industrial and transportation purposes. Because of this, the demand for sour crude oil—a product more readily available in the Middle East—is high. In fact, the Middle East is the main source of oil for most Asian countries.

It is important to clarify the nature of Asian dependence on Middle East oil supplies. Asian countries do not define energy supply security as it relates to the Middle East simply in terms of the availability of crude oil. The lesson learned from the 1991 Gulf War is that Asian countries are more concerned about the vulnerability of the petroleum products trade than of crude oil itself. Were the supply of crude oil from the Middle East to be disrupted or unavailable in sufficient quantities at reasonable prices, Asian countries that plan to construct large petroleum refineries would face serious problems. Changing the input crude oil would require modifying these refineries, which would be both financially costly and technically difficult. Therefore, the success and stability of many Asian downstream projects and activities depend on maintaining supply relationships with Middle East oil producers. This dependence mirrors that of Middle East oil-producing countries, among whose top priorities are securing Asian supply partners, achieving profits from energy-related transactions with Asian customers, and preserving a presence in the Asian oil refining sector.

In South East Asia and China, government-owned petroleum companies and international oil companies are strong in terms of Asian oil trade. Government-owned petroleum companies import oil through direct dealings with oil-producing countries. Depending on the country, an average of 60 to 70 percent of total imports are purchased in this manner, particularly through term contracts. International oil companies have their own supply channels, and their proportion of total imports is approximately 20 percent. With respect to the major oil companies, equity oil is dominant in comparison with the Atlantic oil markets.

Although the demand for petroleum products in Asia has stagnated, the price of Middle East crude oil is not expected to rise sharply, though OPEC expects the marker crude oil price for 1998 to be $15 per barrel. For Middle East oil-producing countries that depend on income from oil exports to provide most of their revenue, the economic crisis in Asia will have led to financial difficulties and a long economic recession. Notwithstanding the importance of these economic conditions in shaping Middle East-Asian energy relations, as will be shown, the structure of oil transactions between the Gulf and Asia might reflect political factors, not simply market forces.

The Politics and Geopolitics of Gulf-Asia Energy Ties
1. The Politics of the Asian Energy Market
The possible liberalization of the energy sector in Asian countries, which

is ultimately a political decision, will have an important bearing on Middle East-Asian energy relations. In 1999, a spot oil exchange market for gasoline, kerosene and crude oil will open in Tokyo. This is a notable event in Asia, for the opening of the market in Japan is expected to promote greater commercialization of petroleum products in the region. Moreover, the Japanese market, unlike the spot markets in New York and London, will be hedging to minimize risk taking and oppose paper barrel speculation.

The spot tradable crude oils are Dubai and Oman. Spot trading of crude oil in Asia, especially in the Singapore market, is currently relatively low, while the Atlantic oil market is active through West Texas Intermediate (WTI) and Brent. If the Japanese market in fact opens, and has the expected positive impact on the rest of the region, oil in Asia will become a much more freely traded commodity.

2. Military Force Projection

Might Gulf-Asia energy ties alter the military doctrines, military modernization programs and force deployments of Asia's regional powers? There is growing speculation that China might deploy the blue sea navy forces in order to defend the sea lanes connecting its coastal waters and the Gulf region through the Indian Ocean. Currently, however, these concerns seem to be misplaced. For the foreseeable future, China's military priorities lie elsewhere. Specifically, Beijing's military preparations are aimed at managing the political-military turmoil on the Korean Peninsula; unifying Taiwan with Mainland China; coping with potentially hostile Vietnam; guarding against possible, if unlikely, military confrontation with India; and preparing for a sharp, though unexpected, downturn in relations with Russia.

The probability that China will deploy its forces in or near the Gulf is low not just because of these overriding security concerns, but also for simple practical reasons. The notion that China will attempt to project force into the Gulf, given US military paramountcy there and the prohibitive expense of doing so, seems to be a possibility as remote as the geographic distance separating China and the Gulf. High-ranking Japanese diplomats almost unanimously agree that, in the coming decades, China will be unwilling or, in any event, unable to deploy large-scale blue sea naval forces far from the Indian Ocean into the Gulf.

Nevertheless, the security linkages between Asian and Gulf regions might take other, potentially harmful and maybe even destabilizing forms. The exchange of oil for arms, or simply the purchase of weapons and weapons technology, raises disturbing possibilities for Asia as well as the Gulf, where dangerous flash points of conflict exist.

3. The Geopolitics of the Energy Crisis in North Korea

The dramatic decrease in petroleum imports from the People's Republic of China and Russia has devastated the energy economy of North Korea. North Korea's single oil refinery has almost shut down its operations because of the shortage of crude oil. There is unconfirmed information that North Korea has negotiated to export military hardware to some countries in the Middle East such as Iran in order to obtain the petroleum needed to offset this shortfall. More clear evidence exists of a North Korean nuclear program, ostensibly to serve the country's energy needs.

These alarming developments illustrate some of the ways in which energy and geopolitics are linked. In order to ameliorate the security threat posed by North Korea's activities, members of the international community have responded with urgency and creativity. In June 1995, the Korea Economic Development Organization (KEDO)—consisting of the United States, Japan and South Korea—decided to provide fuel supplies *gratis* to North Korea until it completes the construction of a light water reactor (LWR) in Tamuho. This agreement is clearly intended to halt the barter practices between North Korea and Middle Eastern countries.

Although the LWR was originally expected to be operational in the year 2003, beginning construction has been delayed. A major stumbling block has been the inability of KEDO to finalize the agreement on the $46 million in financial support required to undertake the project. If this delay persists, the risk of proliferation of nuclear weapons in Asia and the risk to security on the Korean Peninsula will intensify. Furthermore, weapons-for-oil barter contracts between North Korea and Middle Eastern countries may become, if they are not already, the norm rather than the exception.

4. Sino-Gulf Military Cooperation and Power Politics

Although China may be unable or unwilling to project its military forces into the Gulf, it might have some incentive and clearly has the capacity to extend its influence there in other ways. This is to say that North Korea is not the only weapons producer in Asia, nor the only Asian country to have transferred arms to the Middle East. In 1985, for example, China negotiated the sale of the "East Wind" missile to Saudi Arabia. Both before and after this transaction, China sold missiles and other weapons to Iran and Iraq. In fact, during the Iran-Iraq War, China emerged as one of the leading arms exporters to the Gulf; and derived most of its arms export income from Gulf customers.

China's arms exports to the Gulf have declined in the 1990s. There is no evidence of barter arrangements between China and Saudi Arabia, nor between China and Iran; meanwhile, China has strictly observed the UN-based sanctions barring arms transfers to Iraq. Yet, the possibility, however remote, exists that China may some day resume arms deliveries to the Gulf on a significant scale, perhaps in exchange for oil, or simply for strategic purposes, to preserve its supply relationships.

China's activities in the nuclear field provoked as much, indeed more, attention and controversy than its sale of conventional weapons in the Gulf. In 1993, the People's Republic China concluded a technical cooperation agreement with Iran for the construction of a nuclear power plant. However, because of pressure from the United States, which believes that Iran may be involved in suspicious nuclear activities, China and Iran decided to limit their activities to the mutual exchange of engineers and nuclear devices for a period of 10 years. According to some reports, in 1997 China and Iran agreed not to renew the cooperative agreement upon its expiration. Other reports have indicated that in 1993 Iran concluded a similar technical cooperative agreement with Russia. Although neither China nor Iran has issued an official statement concerning this matter, one can speculate that Iran is using nuclear development in a game of power politics with China, Russia, and the United States.

5. Caspian Energy Resources and Geopolitics

For several years, heated negotiations have been under way regarding the construction of oil and gas pipeline routes linking Caspian Basin energy resources to the world market. One of the most contentious debates is about the proposed Baku-Ceyhan route (i.e., a line from Azerbaijan that traverses Turkey and by-passes Iran).

Whether the Baku-Ceyhan project materializes or one of the alternative routes is selected (e.g., via Novorosiisk in Russia or Supsa in Georgia), the main destination for "early oil" from the Caspian will be the European market. This will reduce European dependence on Middle East oil. Although these projects do not specifically aim at the Asian market, international oil companies and their Asian counterparts have measures in place to gain a share of the energy resources of the Caspian Basin. International majors such as Chevron, Mobil, and Japanese *sogo-shosha* like Chu and Ito have incorporated swap plans into their supply arrangements with Middle East customers. These oil swaps are designed to help reduce the long haul transport cost of Caspian crude via the Suez Canal and Indian Ocean to the Asian market. However, it is important to emphasize that these swap deals, will not either by design or in effect, reduce Asian countries' dependence on the Middle East for oil.

Iran is a new and potentially important partner in these swap deals. In late 1997, Iran drafted a plan to swap crude oil extracted from its southern oil fields for equivalent amounts of Caspian crude oil to be shipped to its northern refineries. According to Iran's oil minister, Bijan Namdar-Zannegan, oil originating in the Caspian will serve the domestic market, while oil exported from its southern ports would be destined for the Asian market. These swap deals with Azerbaijan and Kazakhstan could be as large as 1,500 thousand b/d, about enough to absorb the expected incremental crude oil production of the Caspian Sea region.

The gradual improvement of US-Iranian relations has increased the likelihood that these projects will materialize, if not with US endorsement, then possibly with somewhat less vehement opposition. Until recently, the Clinton administration, under pressure from the US Congress, had adhered to tough economic sanctions against Iran, specifically targeting the energy sector. The US government had pressed others, including Japan, to observe these restrictions. Lately, however, buoyed by President Clinton's waiver of secondary sanctions on the French firm, Total, Japanese companies have grown increasingly optimistic that the United States may soon relax, if not remove, sanctions against Iran.

The possibility that the United States may soon reduce or remove the barriers to doing business with Iran has caused Japanese corporate analysts to express relief. This is because they regard access to Caspian energy resources through Iran not just to be more cost-effective but also to be less politically risky than other proposed routes. They view the Black Sea and Mediterranean pipeline routes as potentially unreliable, even if technically feasible and financially affordable. They are concerned that instability in Chechnya and Georgia, or some untoward intervention by Russia, would place oil supplies unnecessarily at risk.

Although US-Iranian relations remain in a delicate transitional state, it is clear that the United States' European allies have become less than ever willing to accede to pressure to isolate Iran economically. Meanwhile, Iran itself is inching forward in accepting foreign involvement in its energy sector. During a London conference held on

July 1-3, 1998, for example, Iran announced an $8 billion oil and gas development plan including onshore areas, and asked for foreign participation. Despite the continuation of US economic sanctions, about 500 representatives from major American, European, and Asian oil companies participated in this conference.

The Iranian invitation to foreign oil firms and the wide interest that it generated by those companies, is significant. It illustrates the degree to which the US-imposed economic sanctions against Iran have become meaningless. It also shows that the Iranian revolution is maturing, for this was the first time since 1979 that the country authorized foreign participation in onshore oil and gas exploration and development. A total of more than 40 gas and oil development projects are included in the plan.

6. US-Japan Security Cooperation
Whereas the United States and Japan do not hold identical views on how to deal with Iran, their security relationship remains solidly intact. Intensifying Gulf-Asia energy interdependence might raise new questions about how to share the responsibilities and costs of securing energy supplies, but it will not jeopardize or fundamentally alter the relationship.

As witnessed during the 1991 Gulf War, the United States' major military deployment to the Gulf was initiated from US mainland bases, with the exception of relatively small operations from Japan. Similarly, in the future, the rapid deployment of US forces could be accomplished primarily from US mainland, rather than from overseas, bases. At the same time, as Gulf-Asia energy ties develop, it may be desirable both from American and Japanese vantage points, to consider how to develop frameworks for securing oil supplies at the sub-regional level.

Conclusion

The growth of crude oil exports from Gulf to Asian countries in recent years has created opportunities for the development of other linkages between the two regions. Some of these are likely to occur in the energy sector, and will be propelled mainly by market forces and by the energy policies of the respective countries. Political factors too—such as improvement in US-Iran relations—might spur further Gulf-Asia energy cooperation. Yet, the interplay of Gulf-Asia energy ties and power politics could also lead to potentially dangerous arms-for-oil transactions. At the present time, North Korea is the player most likely to engage in this activity. Preventing this will require vigilance, creativity, and cooperation.

Energy and Geopolitics: Gulf Perspectives

Regional Cooperation: Untapped Potential

Narsi Ghorban

The strategic and economic importance of the Persian Gulf as a vital source of the world's current and future energy needs is universally recognized. Not surprisingly, therefore, most discussions of "energy security" and the Persian Gulf deal with the relationship between the region's energy resources and the stability of the global economy. This essay, however, focuses on the security dynamics of the region itself. Specifically, it explores the need and the prospects for cooperation among the oil and gas producing states of the Persian Gulf. It argues that cooperation in the energy sector at the regional level is not only possible, but imperative. Furthermore, it argues that this cooperation might constitute an initial step towards the development of comprehensive security arrangements based on mutual economic and strategic interests rather than on the elaborate military presence of outside forces.

Iran and the Persian Gulf

For the past 300 years, Iran has considered the Persian Gulf to be of major significance, strategically and economically. Since the discovery of oil in the early twentieth century and the subsequent development of hydrocarbon resources, Persian Gulf terminals have served as the main outlets for the export of oil from Iran. In addition, substantial reserves of oil and gas have been found and are being exploited in the Iranian sector of the Persian Gulf. For decades, oil revenues have constituted the Iranian government's primary source of foreign exchange earnings, as they have for the region's other producer states. In fact, over the past 25 years, Iran has earned a total of about $350 billion from the export of oil and other goods, and has imported products worth about the same amount, through Persian Gulf ports.

The collapse of the Soviet Union and the emergence of new states in Central Asia and the Caucasus have further enhanced the importance of the Persian Gulf. For these new states, the Gulf represents an alternative commercial passageway. Iran is favorably situated to link these states with those of the Persian Gulf. Iran's cultural ties with the people of West and Central Asia, which have been revived since the demise of the Soviet Union, provide an additional basis for regional cooperation.

The potential benefits of cooperation among the oil and gas producers and consumers in the region cannot, indeed must not, be overlooked. Unless these states cooperate with each other in the development and delivery of the Caspian Basin's oil and gas to external markets, these resources will become yet another source of conflict in the region. Regional oil and gas trade projects are cost effective alternatives to competitive, possibly conflict-inducing, national strategies of resource development. In this respect, oil swaps with the Caspian states and gas cooperation between Iran, Qatar, Turkmenistan, and Kazakhstan.

Oil Swaps

Iran is a major energy producer and consumer. Iran produces about 5 million barrels of oil per day (mb/d) and consumes nearly 1.6 mb/d. Whereas most of Iran's oil and gas fields are located in the south, consumption is concentrated in the central and northern parts of the country. Over 0.7 mb/d of oil is pumped to from the southern oil fields to the refineries of Arak, Isfahan, Tabriz, and Tehran. Most of the 45 billion cubic meters of gas consumed each year (bncm/y) is also pumped from the south to the north. The international oil companies recognize the advantages for using Iran to export part of the oil produced in the Caspian Basin. In fact, in the absence of US sanctions on Iran, most of the early oil from the Caspian Basin would have been exported from Iran.

The main economic advantages of oil exports via Iran are based on its geographic location, growing domestic petroleum product demand, and extensive network of crude oil, gas and petroleum product pipelines. Iran's common border with Turkmenistan is nearly 1,500 kilometers long. Iran also borders Armenia, Azerbaijan, Nakhichevan, and Turkey. Iran's oil and gas pipeline system lies within 200 kilometers of all of these countries. Iran's demand for petroleum products is primarily in the northern half of the country, which is has a population of about 50 million and generally has cold winters. If the present trend in consumption of petroleum products continues, Iran will have to build more refineries in this part of the country.

The Tabriz and Tehran refineries are the most logical outlets for crude oil from Azerbaijan, Kazakhstan, and Turkmenistan. The idea of an "oil swap" is to use crude oil from these countries to supply the above-mentioned refineries in exchange for crude oil from the Persian Gulf. This arrangement would be the quickest, cheapest solution to the problem of exporting some of the oil produced in the region. This project could be achieved in three phases.

Phase I of the oil swap project would entail construction of a 390- km, 32-inch diameter pipeline from Neka to the Tehran refinery. This pipeline would be capable of transporting over 300,000 b/d of Caspian oil from Neka to the Tehran (200,00 b/d) and Tabriz (100,000 b/d) refineries. The National Iranian Oil Company (NIOC) has in fact invited international companies to bid for this project, which will be awarded by the end of 1998 and is expected to be operational in less than two years. The project will require the construction of storage facilities at Neka as well as modification of the Tabriz and Tehran refineries. The existing product pipeline between Neka and Tehran has a capacity of 40,000 b/d, which could be expanded to 120,000 b/d in a relatively short time. This line is currently used to swap oil under separate agreements with the British Monument Oil and Gas Company, Irish Dragon Oil Company, and Kazakh National Oil Company.

Phase II of the project would entail swapping additional quantities of Caspian oil by supplying the Arak and Isfahan refineries, which have capacities of 150,000 b/d and 220,000 b/d, respectively. This will require consideration of a number of options. A pipeline from Baku to Tabriz, for example, could utilize the existing 42-inch diameter gas pipeline between Astara and Baku, (built in the late 1970s) to carry Iranian gas to the former Soviet Union. From Astara, a 250-km pipeline parallel to the existing gas line to Tabriz can bring 250,000 b/d of oil to the Tabriz refinery. The existing pipelines between Tabriz and Tehran will then transport 120,000 b/d of oil to the network, which, if reversed, could carry this oil, as well as some of the oil from Phase I, to the Arak and Isfahan refineries.

A second alternative is to build a pipeline to connect the port of Anzali to the point where crude oil pipelines currently carry 110,000 b/d of oil to the Tabriz refinery. From this point, 110,000 b/d of oil could go north to the Tabriz facility, while a similar amount could be pumped south to the Tehran installation. Once this project is completed and oil from the Caspian Basin is supplied to the Tabriz and Tehran refineries, the pipelines that now bring oil to these refineries would be empty, and could therefore be reversed to carry more oil from the Caspian Basin to the Arak and Isfahan refineries in Phase II.

The cost of Phases I and II is estimated at about $750 million. The network could absorb nearly 700,000 b/d of oil from the West and Central Asian countries. It must be noted that Iranian companies, which are already actively engaged in the Iranian oil industry, could do most of this work; therefore, the bulk of expenditure would be in local currency.

Phase III of the project would involve construction of additional pipelines in order to bring more oil from the Caspian Basin to the Iranian oil network. This oil would be transported to the Kharg oil export terminal, where there is ample capacity available for shipment of oil to international markets. Completion of this phase would depend upon several factors: the oil production capacity of the Caspian Basin; the building of alternative pipelines; and regional political developments. In this scenario, the possibility of transferring additional Caspian crude oil via a direct pipeline from Turkmenistan to Iran must be studied. Conceivably, another 800,000 b/d of oil could be transported under Phase III, bringing the total to nearly 1.5 mb/d. The associated costs of this third phase are likely to be higher than the two earlier stages of the project, but will be much lower than competitive schemes currently under consideration.

There are several advantages of an oil swap arrangement of the type described above. First, Caspian producers could begin to export their crude oil within a relatively short period of time. Second, they could avoid the large capital expenditures required to construct pipelines through different countries. Third, because this kind of swap arrangement does not require the consent of any third country and because Iran would be the end user, there would be a strong incentive for all of the participants to work towards the timely completion of the project. Fourth, the relatively low costs involved would ensure the maximum return per barrel to the producers, while Iran could benefit from swap fees, low oil transportation costs, and the economic benefits stemming from building the infrastructure required for these projects. Finally, a swap arrangement would allow Caspian crude oil to compete in the markets of the Far East, which are expected to show substantial growth in the coming years. In contrast, oil delivered to the Black Sea or Mediterranean Sea would compete with Russian, Iraqi, Syrian, Egyptian, North African, and North Sea crude oil. Moreover, oil routes to the Black Sea would have to pass through the Bosporous Straits, raising transportation costs and probably sparking opposition from Turkey based on environmental concerns.

Regional Gas Cooperation

Most of the recent studies on world energy market trends indicate that the Middle East and Central Asia will play a significant role in the trade of natural gas, particularly in the Indian subcontinent, Turkey, Armenia, Georgia, and some parts of Europe. Cooperation among the major gas-producing states is the most economical way to develop gas resources and construct transmission networks for gas utilization in the long term. Iran, Turkmenistan, and Kazakhstan could cooperate in developing a major pipeline network capable of carrying gas from these countries to the regional and international markets. This will avoid simultaneous development of large pipelines and LNG projects for the same markets. Qatar could also be connected to Iran's pipeline network by constructing a small pipeline from its North Dome field to the Iranian port of Assaloieh.

Iran has the world's second largest gas reserves after Russia; moreover, by reason of geography, Iran is uniquely situated to serve as a link between the Caspian Sea countries and the Persian Gulf states. Iran has common borders with Pakistan and Turkey, two countries which are expected to be major gas importers in the coming decades. In addition, Iran's gas pipeline network already extends from the Persian Gulf in the south, to the Caspian Sea and Azerbaijan in the north. Iran's existing East-West pipeline system extends from Sarakhs at the Turkmenistan border, to Rezaieh near the Turkish border. This gas pipeline network consists of nearly 4,000 kms. of major lines (between 20-56 inches in diameter) and over 10,000 kms. of high-pressure pipelines capable of carrying over 70 billion cubic meters of gas per year (bncm/y) for domestic consumption and injection into oil fields. Additional pipelines are under construction to bring more gas from the South Pars gas field in the Persian Gulf to the major centers of consumption.

In 1997, Iran's gas network was connected to that of Turkmenistan; and 4 bncm of Turkmen gas will be pumped to Iran this winter. The amount of gas from Turkmenistan will be increased to 9 bncm/y in the coming years. The Royal Dutch Shell Oil Company is studying the possibility of building a huge gas transmission network linking Turkmenistan, Iran, and Turkey. If this project materializes, the pipeline will eventually supply Turkey with 30 bncm/y of gas from Turkmenistan. By expanding existing pipelines and building some new ones, Kazakhstan could easily be connected to this network.

Recent political developments in the region have not been conducive to the development of major gas projects that might involve India and Pakistan. Due to the political situation in Southwest Asia, Unocal has suspended its controversial plan to supply gas to Pakistan via Afghanistan. Given these circumstances, the logical approach to supply gas to the Indian subcontinent is initially through cooperation between Turkmenistan and Iran, and subsequently with the involvement of other producers. A gas pipeline of 42-inches in diameter from Turkmenistan's fields at the border with Iran could be constructed, joining the proposed pipeline from Iran to Pakistan near Zahedan. Iran's industrial infrastructure, engineering capability, and experiences work force would ensure the rapid and economical completion of this project.

There are several major advantages of cooperation among gas producers to establish a regional gas network. First, this network would draw gas from various suppliers and deliver it to a multitude of customers, thereby reducing the risk of excessive dependence for both producers and consumers. Second, it will preclude the need for each country to make a massive capital outlay to build its own pipeline. Third, this project is consistent with the environmental objectives of all the countries concerned. For this reason, the project might attract support from the World Bank and other international financial institutions. Finally, this project might lead to the formation of other trans-national economic linkages, and ultimately contribute to regional stability and prosperity.

Conclusion

Energy cooperation between Iran and West and Central Asian countries is the most logical and economical approach to export oil and gas from the Caspian Basin. Oil swap deals between Iran, Azerbaijan, Turkmenistan, and Kazakhstan are potentially valuable instruments to achieve this end. Similarly, regional cooperation among gas producers is both technically feasible and economical.

Capitalizing on this opportunity depends as much, if not more, on political will and policy capacity as on geological and economic factors. The governments of the countries concerned—particularly that of Iran, which literally and figuratively is a central player in a putative regional energy network—must enact legislation designed to encourage domestic and foreign investors to participate in these projects. Furthermore, these governments must launch a coordinated political campaign to ensure that all elements within their governments understand and cooperate in the implementation of these projects. Finally, they must jointly approach international financial institutions to obtain support for these projects.

The land-locked countries of the Caspian Basin need secure outlets for their oil and gas exports. The energy markets of the Far East and Indian subcontinent, though currently languishing due to financial and political problems, will resume their expansion in the coming decades. Iran is a natural energy corridor linking the Caspian Basin and Persian Gulf with the markets to the east. The shared economic benefits that are likely to result from building a regional oil and gas network that traverses Iranian territory, along with its possible salutary effect on regional stability, are considerable. Arguably, the biggest obstacle to undertaking these endeavors is the political pressure to by-pass Iran.

Market Myths and Political Realities

Issam Al-Chalabi

Since the November 1997 OPEC summit meeting in Jakarta, oil-producing countries have struggled to prevent prices from further decline. This crisis is the worst one faced by oil producers since the crash of 1986 and perhaps since the early 1970s. To some degree, the Organization of Petroleum Exporting Countries (OPEC) exacerbated this crisis by declaring a 10 percent increase in production (amounting to 2.5 mb/d) at a time when the world oil market was already over-supplied.

During the seven-month period following the Jakarta summit at which this decision was taken, OPEC scrambled to arrest the crisis. OPEC's remedy for the crisis was essentially to reverse the course it had set at Jakarta. A succession of OPEC meetings—held in Riyadh, Vienna, Amsterdam and again in Vienna—culminated in an agreement to cut back production by 2.6 mb/d, with an additional .5 mb/d production decrease expected from non-OPEC producers. At least temporarily, this appears to have prevented the further collapse of oil prices.

Yet, the problems and challenges faced by oil producers, particularly the Gulf states (whose combined output constitutes 70 percent of OPEC's total production) are nonetheless acute. To a significant degree, these problems are connected to the current situation in Asia. From the mid-1980s until one year ago, the Asian "tiger" economies had, to use a metaphor, roamed freely in the woods. Since 1997, however, they have been crippled and caged.

The intersection of the oil price and Asian financial crises raises questions about two issues, one related to the nature of Gulf-Asia "energy interdependence," and the other concerned with the meaning of "energy security" as it applies to the Gulf and Asia-Pacific regions. Were the energy relationships that had developed between these two regions over the past decade merely transitory? Does the term "energy security" simply refer to the security of supply for Asian oil-consuming countries?

Gulf-Asia Energy Interdependence

Gulf-Asia energy interdependence is a permanent structural feature

71

of the world energy market. The energy assets of Gulf producers and the future energy requirements of Asia-Pacific countries are complementary. Furthermore, given long-term global energy trends, Gulf oil producers have no viable replacement for the Asian energy market, while Asia-Pacific countries have no practical substitute for Gulf suppliers.

During the 1980s and 1990s, Asian countries grew increasingly dependent on oil supplies from the Gulf. This dependency stemmed from the limitation of reserves in Southeast Asia, the proximity of the Gulf compared to other oil and gas producing regions, well-established and efficient maritime transportation systems, low-cost and diverse grades of oil. It also stemmed from a common interest between Gulf oil suppliers and Asian oil customers to develop mutual trade and investment both within and outside the energy sector. Over the years, political and military problems temporaily interrupted oil supplies from the Gulf. In response to these developments and at the encouragement of the International Monetary Fund (IMF), Asian countries sought to diversify their sources of supply. Nevertheless, all Asian countries continue to rely primarily on oil supplies from the Gulf; moreover, the dominance of oils supplies from the Gulf continues to be factored into their energy strategies.

Despite the decline in Asian energy demand growth from an average of 7.4 percent to about 3 to 4 percent, most observers believe that, in the coming years, Asia's energy demand will continue to be the most important element in world energy demand. While global energy demand is expected to rise at an annual rate of around 1.5 to 2 percent, Asia's growth is expected to settle at about 4 percent. By the year 2010, Asia will account for over 55 percent of the global increase in oil demand in spite of the fact that oil's share in the total energy mix is expected to decline slightly from the current level of 40 percent. For many years to come, Asia will play a crucial role in world demand for oil, and in demand for oil from the Gulf in particular. For this reason, it is as important to Gulf producers that Asian countries overcome their current economic problems as it is important to Asian countries to gain long-term guaranteed access to oil supplies from the Gulf.

The total oil reserves of the Gulf region is estimated at 670 billion barrels. This represents 94.4 percent of the Middle East's, and 64.6 percent of the world's, proven reserves. According to the British Petroleum Company (BP), the Gulf's oil reserves are divided among the "Seven Brothers" as follows (in billion of barrels): Saudi Arabia (261.5), Iraq (112.0), the United Arab Emirates (97.8), Kuwait (96.5), Iran (93.0), Oman (5.1), and Qatar (3.7). Of these, the "Big Five" possess a combined

661 billion barrels of oil in reserve. This constitutes 98.6 of Gulf, 98 percent of Middle East, and 63.7 percent of world reserves. Significantly, at present rates of production, the Seven Brothers enjoy a reserves/production (R/P) ratio of about 93 years, while the Big Five have an RP ratio of more than 100 years, compared with an RP ratio of 42 years for the whole world.

Gulf-Asia energy interdependence has increased in the gas sector as well. Asian countries have considered adopting, and in some cases, have already begun to implement more stringent environmental policies. Among other things, this has led to increased Asian demand for gas and corresponding efforts to find secure supplies. Gulf gas producing countries have welcomed these developments. They have sought Asian investment partners in order to expand their gas industries. In fact, in recent years, Asian countries such as Japan and South Korea have engaged in most of the major gas development projects in the Gulf, including those in Dubai, Abu Dhabi, and Oman.

Gulf countries possess huge gas reserves and are therefore well-positioned to help meet Asia's future gas requirements. In fact, of the world's estimated 145 trillion cubic meters (tcm) of proven gas reserves, the Gulf share is about 49 tcm, or 33.8 percent. After Russia, which has about 48 tcm of gas, Iran and Qatar have the world's second and third largest reserves, totaling 23 tcm and 8.5 tcm, respectively.

Sources of Energy Supply Insecurity

1. The Myth of Resource Scarcity

Forecasters have always been wrong about the availability of oil. They have consistently underestimated reserves as well as human ingenuity. Although oil is a finite resource, it is not a scarce one. Oil, especially oil from the Gulf, will be available for far longer than some analysts have claimed. The danger of "oil scarcity," that is, of exhaustion of the world's oil supplies, is miniscule. Similarly, predictions that Caspian Basin energy resources will significantly reduce the Gulf's share of global energy supplies does not withstand close scrutiny.

In 1973, prior to the establishment of the International Energy Agency (IEA), the Club of Rome predicted that the world would face an oil "resource constraint" by the end of the century. At that time, they estimated the world's reserves at 600 billion barrels, with an oil reserve-to-production (R/P) ratio of 29 years. In 1980, oil supplies were expected to increase from 66 million b/d in 1979 to 70 million b/d in the year 2000, while oil demand was expected to rise to about 60 million b/d by the year

2000. The IEA's 1987 Energy Outlook projected a demand increase of 4.8 million b/d for the period 1986-95.

Yet, all of these forecasts turned out to be wide of the mark. As the end of the century approaches, taking into account cumulative world production of about 500 billion barrels during the period 1973-96, we still have over 1,000 billion barrels, with a production lifespan of a further 42 years. Current supply stands at about 75 million b/d, while demand is about 74 million b/d. World oil supplies have therefore turned out to be far more elastic than many had predicted.

Many claims about the possible impact of Caspian Basin energy supplies on the energy market are likewise exagerrated. It is true that some time in the next decade the Caspian countries will take their place among the world's major oil and gas producers. In its report *The Caspian Sea Region*, the International Energy Agency (IEA) estimated the total *proven* oil reserves of the Caspian area to be between 15 and 29 billion barrels, compared with reserves of 22 billion barrels for the United States and 17 billion barrels for the North Sea. The same report estimated the Caspian's *possible* oil reserves at 163 billion barrels, though one must emphasize that this oil has less than a 50 percent recovery rate. Comparing these IEA figures with those previously mentioned for the Gulf, it is clear that Caspian producers may some day emerge as significant suppliers of oil and gas; however, they will not supplant the Big Five Gulf producers in the global energy market. Moreover, for the Caspian producer countries to realize their full potential, they will have to overcome a number of persistent technological, financial, and other problems.

In future, world oil supplies will continue to be sufficient to meet world demand. In all likelihood, there will always be additional quantities of proven reserves to substitute partially or totally for amounts that are consumed. These additional supplies will come from new discoveries in current producer countries and existing fields. Low costs of production and improved technologies that have yet to be applied in most producer countries, will be an important factor in finding new reserves. Lower prices might dampen investment in exploration activities, but only temporarily. Present semi-depleted fields will come to life, as recovery factors as low as 10 percent in the Middle East, gradually improve. Iraq is a good illustration. Iraq's current proven reserves are estimated at 112 billion barrels. At the present time, Iraq has many virgin areas and low recovery rates in existing producing fields. Many believe, however, that Iraq's possible reserves might exceed 300 billion barrels.

In the context of the world energy market, Gulf producers will continue to be "residual suppliers." Gulf oil will continue to be the largest by any standard of measurement, though there will be other regions that produce oil and gas. Given that OPEC will continue to be price conscious, other producers will feel free to market their oil. This will leave OPEC to fill the gap, whether its members like it or not.

2. Regional Conflict and Supply Disruptions

Although energy insecurity is unlikely to stem from a scarcity of oil, it might well result from disruptions of supply. In the comning years, as in the recent past, regional conflict poses the biggest threat to the flow of oil supplies from the Gulf.

Islam is the predominant faith of all seven of the Gulf oil-producing countries. The Arabic language and Arab culture is shared by six of them, while five are members of the Gulf Cooperation Council (GCC). Yet despite these commonalities, during the twentieth century, relations between these neighboring countries have been plagued by mistrust and periodic conflict. The Gulf's turbulent recent history and the various unresolved issues of dispute among the Gulf states provide little confidence in the possibility of a tranquil future. In turn, this has a direct bearing on the prospects for maintaining secure oil supplies from the Gulf.

The eight-year Iran-Iraq War (1980-1988) left deep scars that are likely to affect relations between these countries for many years to come. The war was enormously costly to Iran and Iraq in human lives as well as in damage to the physical infrastructure. This war also had an important regional dimension. Although not belligerents *per se*, the other Gulf states were nonetheless affected by the war; moreover, through their financial support for Iraq and the roles they played in the oil market, they were directly involved in the conflict.

When the Iran-Iraq War broke out, members of the GCC were ready to compensate for the sizable loss of oil to the world market caused by the conflict. Yet, contrary to expectations, oil prices continued to decline. In 1984-85, OPEC reduced its ceiling to about 16 million b/d, as oil prices fell to single digits. What would have happened to the already over-supplied world oil market had an additional four million barrels per day of Iranian and Iraqi oil been available?

Today, the overall geopolitical situation in the Middle East, especially in the Gulf, is volatile. Two of the Gulf's leading oil producers are under sanctions. A prolonged stalemate in the Arab-Israeli peace process has contributed to regional tension. The governments of all of the Gulf's oil-producing states face demographic and budgetary problems, which have been compounded by a prolonged period of low oil prices with no relief in sight. Amidst this general climate of pressure and hostility in the Gulf, there are specific flashpoints of potential conflict. Because of the lingering animosity between Iran and Iraq, a renewal of conflict between these countries cannot be ruled out.

Potential sources of interstate conflict are not limited to the residual problems between Iran and Iraq. There are a number of territorial and other disputes that might lead to military confrontation and possibly to oil supply disruptions. The dispute between Iran and the United Arab Emirates (UAE) on sovereignty over the Tunbs islands and Abu Musa is like a time bomb that could, with some provocation from outside forces, develop into a major military conflict involving other Gulf states. Qatar and Bahrain are at odds, and have been engaged in a costly arms race, over ownership of the oil-rich Hawar Island. It is not inconceivable that the large US military presence in the Gulf, coupled with Iran's uneasy relations with some of its Arab Gulf neighbors, might produce an incident which might then escalate into a military confrontation.

Conclusion

Oil export volumes from the Gulf are expected to rise by about 8 million b/d over the next 20 years. Of this amount, about 83 percent is expected to be directed towards Asia, particularly to China, Japan, Korea, and others. Asia is a region of great importance to the global oil industry, to OPEC and to Gulf producers. After all, there will be some 400 million Asians in the next 15-20 years.

As a result of the 1991 Gulf War and UN-mandated economic sanctions, Iraq's energy industry and related infrastructure has suffered severe damage and disrepair. To restore Iraq's production capacity to pre-Gulf War levels, more time, investment, and foreign support will be required than many observers have suggested. Asian countries thus have an opportunity and, given their energy needs, have an interest in contributing to the future reconstruction of Iraq's energy industry.

Implications for US Policy

Opportunities and Challenges

Geoffrey Kemp

The growing reliance of Asian countries on oil and gas supplies from the Persian Gulf poses opportunities as well as challenges for US policy. Although oil has always been an important strategic commodity, it was the 1973 Arab-Israeli war and the subsequent Arab oil embargo that focused American attention on both the importance and vulnerability of Persian Gulf energy supplies. The issue assumed strategic dimensions for three reasons. First, the emergence of the Organization of Petroleum Exporting Countries (OPEC) as a powerful counterweight to the OECD countries prompted talk about a fundamental redistribution of international power with the oil exporting countries becoming, in effect, the world's bankers. Second, the crisis coincided with the growth of the Soviet Union's military power projection capabilities and raised fears that in a future world crisis, Moscow and its far-flung surrogates would be in a strong position to interdict vital oil and raw materials supplies to the West from the Middle East and Africa. This prompted countervailing military strategies to protect oil supplies, especially from the Persian Gulf, and to defend sea lines of communication (SLOCs) across the world's oceans. A third factor was the rise of the environmental movement and the publication of several influential doomsday books that predicted the "limits to growth" and the need to abandon the ethos of economic expansion that was the engine behind the success of the OECD countries.

The gloomy scenarios of the 1970s did not materialize for a number of disparate but important reasons. The OPEC cartel and the validity of the "limits to growth" thesis lost their potency as a result of wise decisions by the Western powers to conserve energy through economic incentives, the development of new oil sources outside the Middle East, the establishment of strategic petroleum stockpiles and sharing agreements, and investments in new technologies to speed efficiency and adaptation. The other momentous event, of course, was the collapse of the Soviet Union and Warsaw Pact in the late 1980s, which rendered obsolete the notion of a great power confrontation over the sea lines of communication.

The resilience of the West to energy disruption was tested in the mid-1980s during the Iran-Iraq War when Iraq embarked on a "tanker war" to curtail Iran's oil exports, and Iran responded by attacking Arab tankers. At that time the oil market was saturated due to slackened demand from the West (which was experiencing an economic recession) and abundant new sources of supply. Tanker sinkings in the Persian Gulf that ten years earlier would have triggered panic became part of the daily violence of that war and had little, if any, impact on world oil prices.

However, in August 1990 a serious threat to global order loomed when Saddam Hussein suddenly invaded Kuwait and moved his forces to the Saudi border. Had Saddam's armies continued into the Saudi oil fields, it is doubtful that Operation Desert Shield and Desert Storm could have been mounted. Under those circumstances, Saddam would have been in a position to dictate peace terms to the Arab world and control the price of oil, at least for a short period. Most ominously, he would have been able to pay off Iraq's huge war debt and complete his nuclear weapons program. With a full range of weapons of mass destruction, a large army and the ability to control Arabia's oil reserves, Iraq would have become a regional superpower. This would have had huge consequences for the Middle East and beyond.

Fortunately, Saddam Hussein miscalculated. The massive Western response was made possible by the cooperation of the Arab countries, especially Egypt and Saudi Arabia. Among other things, these countries provided an excellent forward area base structure that the United States had developed in the 1970s and 1980s to meet a potential Soviet challenge to the Persian Gulf. Thus, the 1970s crisis had led to a level of military preparedness that was essential to the success of Desert Storm.

Growing Energy Demand

By the year 2020, world demand for energy could be triple what it was in 1970. The increased demand will be met primarily by oil, natural gas, and coal. The energy needs of the newly industrializing countries could more than double by the year 2010. Correspondingly, world demand for oil will grow, and is projected to increase from 71.6 million barrels per day (mbd) in 1997 to exceed 115 mbd by the year 2020. In 1995, the OECD countries used two-thirds of the world's oil supplies; however, over the next two decades, they are expected to account for only one-third of the increase in demand.

A number of unforeseen developments could alter projected energy demand. These include global economic recession or even depression;

changing taxation and subsidy policies in key energy consuming countries motivated partly by environmental concerns; and radical breakthroughs in energy efficient, cost effective technologies. These caveats aside, it is possible to outline the general trends for the next 15 to 20 years. First, for the foreseeable future, there is enough oil in many parts of the world to meet global demand. The problem is getting the oil out of the ground and guaranteeing its distribution to the market place at an acceptable price. The primary obstacles to increased access to this oil are political, economic and logistical rather than geological. Furthermore, while the world is awash in oil (and coal and natural gas), some of the most promising sources for new production are located in two of the most politically unstable regions on earth, the Persian Gulf and the Caspian Basin. These regions contain over two-thirds of the world's proven oil reserves and possibly forty percent of the world's natural gas reserves. The Persian Gulf alone is capable of meeting much of the growing demand for energy in the industrial world.

It is possible that oil might become available from the other major reserve regions including Siberia, Western China, West Africa, and South America. However, political and economic costs involved in developing these regions are also likely to limit their contribution to the market within the next 15 years. Although technologies are being developed for more cost-effective fuel cells and electric vehicles, few believe that this will substantially reduce demand for gasoline for the internal combustion in the next 15 years. Natural gas is becoming an increasingly important component of world energy because it is clean and efficient. Nevertheless, getting it to market is much more difficult than oil. There is no benchmark price for gas, and the investment costs for transportation are huge.

Sources of Energy Supply Insecurity

Of the possible threats to energy supplies (particularly oil) that have given rise to the generic term "energy security," I shall discuss three. Any one of these threats could change the overall world energy situation and, in certain circumstances, alter the balance of power.

1. Physical Disruption of the Flow of Oil

The interruption of oil supplies from the Gulf could have an immediate impact on the price of oil, which would in turn adversely affect the world economy. The extent of these effects would depend on which countries' oil were disrupted, the time of the year and duration of this occurrence, and the relationship of demand to supply levels at the time. There is a temptation to use the 1990 invasion of Kuwait and the ensuing embargo on Iraq as models to construct future worst-case scenarios. Yet, there are possible scenarios whose consequences could be far more detrimental to the world economy than these. Were Saudi Arabia some day to be engulfed in a civil war, the conflict might interfere with, or interrupt, oil production operations. Were a full-scale military confrontation to take place in the Gulf, the Strait of Hormuz might prove impassable for oil tanker traffic. Both of these scenarios are plausible.

2. Oil Production Capacity Restraints

Although the Gulf has an enormous amount of oil that can be extracted at reasonable costs both onshore and offshore, producers must continue to invest in plant and equipment to keep up with demand. Investment shortfalls are possible due to several factors: a) budgetary strains during this protracted period of low oil prices and low oil revenues; b) the "over-supply" syndrome or tendency to postpone capacity expansion, given the oil glut; and c) the relatively uncongenial, "statist" climate for foreign investment. Thus, the "capacity problem" is an "investment problem." In turn, these problems are compounded, if not caused, by a combination of adverse market forces and poor policy choices.

3. The Emergence of a Hostile Regional Hegemon

This case is, of course, a variant of the 1990-91 crisis over Iraq. As long as Persian Gulf oil remains such a critical ingredient in world energy supplies, any hostile power that controls the Arabian peninsula would have the potential to influence oil prices in an upward direction and to use income generated from oil revenues to expand military arsenals, including weapons of mass destruction. Thus, fears about the re-emergence of Saddam Hussein's Iraq or Iranian hegemony over the Gulf are very real. Concern about the behavior of Iran's leaders continues to be one reason why the United States has made great efforts to limit Iran's energy production and its capacity to control access routes. While the wisdom of this strategy is frequently challenged, its rationale still commands strong support in Washington. Anticipation of this case is the primary motive for the continued US military presence in the Gulf.

The Gulf-Asia Energy Security Nexus

Over the past decade, the Asia-Pacific region emerged as the fastest growing market for Gulf producers. Furthermore, according to numerous studies and projections, this region is expected to emerge as the leading market for Gulf oil supplies early in the next century. The Asia-Pacific region's customers for Gulf energy supplies include traditional US allies like Japan and South Korea, as well as a long-time nemesis of the United States, North Korea. They also include regional powers such as China and India, with which the United States has stable, but complicated, relations.

What impact will Asia's need for oil and natural gas have on international security? This question has generated a cottage industry of studies that range from the apocalyptic to the complacent. The magnitude of Asian energy demand will be determined by the growth rates of Asian economies, which at present are much slower than forecast a year ago. However, even under slow growth scenarios, the energy needs of the largest countries in this region will far exceed current capacities. Indeed, countries like China and India already face severe energy shortfalls which must be remedied if high growth is to be restored to their economies. If automobile usage in China and India continues to expand, demand for petroleum will soar. Most of this petroleum will eventually have to be imported.

What beneficial or dangerous potential consequences for US interests in the Gulf might spring from the eventual resumption of growth of Asian dependence on Gulf energy sources?

1. Opportunities

In some respects, the growth of Gulf-Asia energy ties might be a blessing in disguise. US policymakers might be wise to encourage more extensive energy interdependence between these two regions. Increasing energy demand by Asian countries is spurred by economic growth, which is a generally positive development. However, for two of Asia's largest energy customers—China and India—coal is the leading primary energy source. The continuation, or worse, an increase of coal consumption poses major environmental hazards. One way to mitigate these problems is for Asian countries to shift to greater reliance on oil and gas. Yet, it will require an infusion of considerable capital and technology needed to accomplish this. Over the next 20 years, China might need to invest as much as one trillion dollars in energy capacity, particularly electricity-generating capacity. The figure is about $500 billion for India. It is in the interest of the United States (and Japan) to help China and India obtain this investment capital.

2. Risks

The energy relationships between Asian and Gulf countries might be accompanied by, or might spawn, other linkages. Overall, increasingly close ties between the Gulf, China, and the Indian sub-continent might dramatically transform the political and economic geography of the Middle East region. Although the political impact of these ties on the Gulf and on US interests is not clear, it will not necessarily prove to be positive.

There are several kinds of potential concerns to the United States: those at the state level and those at the societal level. The recent nuclear weapons tests in India and Pakistan, Iran's test firing of a missile with an 800-mile range, concern about Iraq's weapons of mass destruction and the continuing Arab-Israeli conflict are vivid reminders of the instability and dangers in inter-state relations in the region. The fact that China has provided Iran and Pakistan with missile technology suggests to some that its intentions are strategic, as well as commercial.

At the societal level, linkages between the Gulf and South Asia in the labor sector, forged during the oil boom of the 1970s, already exist. The key factors responsible for this—the proximity of South Asia to the Gulf, and the disparity in population size and per capita income—are fundamentally unchanged. Some of the possible negative political consequences of the presence of a large Asian labor force in the Gulf have already been realized. Riots by expatriate workers in Dubai in 1992, for example, provided the most serious internal challenge in the emirate's history. This unrest was inflamed by the Hindu-Muslim dispute over the destruction of the Ayodha mosque in India.

3. Constraints

Whatever precise form these risks might take, US policymakers must consider the diplomatic, economic and military tools that might be required to respond to them. Although the US enjoys unprecedented latitude to act unilaterally, it also faces a number of constraints. These take three forms: 1) dissipation of the post-Cold War international climate of "consensuality;" 2) the predisposition of the key Asian states to opt for "national" approaches to secure energy supplies; and 3) multilateral constraints, such as UN Security Council resolutions.

In areas which require the cooperation of others (e.g., arms control regimes, economic sanctions, a massive military intervention) the United States cannot count on cooperation from the international community, as, for instance during the 1990-91 Gulf crisis and war. At that time, there were numerous factors that enabled the United States to act decisively and effectively. President George Bush was able to orchestrate a unique coalition against Saddam Hussein owing to the exceptional circumstances of that moment. Iraq's invasion of Kuwait was such a flagrant violation of the most basic principle of international relations that near unanimous votes condemning Iraq and applying sanctions at the United Nations were possible. For the first time since World War II, the United States and the Soviet Union found themselves on the same side concerning the use of force in the Middle East. Most Arab countries supported the United States, including Syria. On the domestic front, President Bush was able to secure Congressional and public support for military action.

Encountering such favorable conditions the next time there is a crisis in the Gulf are unlikely. Since 1991, the crises with Iraq have been far less consensual. In the February 1998 crisis over UNSCOM weapons inspections, only British Prime Minister Tony Blair was willing to offer combat forces alongside those of the United States. New Gulf crises are likely to be ambiguous in terms of who the culprit is, and this will make it much more difficult to reach a consensus at the United Nations or elsewhere over how to respond.

The United States has, and, in the foreseeable future, will continue to have the military capability to deter high-level threats that could affect the security of Gulf countries and therefore the security of the supply of oil. Nevertheless, the United States has little control over the internal security problems that these Gulf countries will face in the coming decades. These threats relate to autocracy, corruption, income maldistribution, migration issues, and extremism. Compounding these problems are low oil prices and the erosion of the state's capacity to fund entitlements programs. It is not unreasonable to assume that another crisis will come at a time when the oil market is a bit tighter, and that key Asian allies and China will be much less willing to accept American leadership concerning crisis management.

There are different hypotheses regarding how Asian dependence on Gulf energy supplies might affect the security of the Gulf and US interests there. Some argue that market forces will be the primary determinant of stable energy supplies, and that there will be no long-term supply shortages. The basis of this argument is that oil is a fungible, universal commodity that commands a worldwide benchmark price. Thus, China, Japan, and Korea will always find oil, but they will have to compete for it on the open market. If supplies are disrupted from one region, such as the Gulf, prices will rise in the short run until the market adjusts.

Others, however, are skeptical that the leaders of the Asian countries will quickly and fully embrace this logic. They doubt that all of them will have the foresight and the capacity to entrust their national interests to market mechanisms. They argue that the world is not run by rational economists. Furthermore, they contend, although the market tends to work efficiently, it does not take into account the strong diversities of national opinion that prevail throughout Asia and that different Asian countries will adopt different methods for dealing with their energy security problem. The Chinese leadership in particular, with its deep suspicion of the United States, will be extremely wary of growing dependency on regions as unstable as the Persian Gulf. For this reason its leaders, especially its military leaders, will take steps to ensure that China is not vulnerable to either interference with its energy supplies by a potentially hostile power such as the United States, or complications arising in a region like the Middle East over which it presently has no control. Over the next 20-25 years, the net result could be the emergence of a Chinese blue water navy. This would clearly have an impact on its Asian neighbors, particularly India.

Finally, we should not take for granted the willingness of the United States to serve indefinitely as the protector of the Persian Gulf. If, in the future, the American economy were to be less strong than it is today, and if American forces deployed to the Gulf and elsewhere were to sustain higher numbers of casualties than they recently have, US congressional and public support for the US military presence in the Gulf could conceivably erode. This might come about as the result of a messy conflict in the Gulf, one in which the United States finds itself alone or with few allies. If this coincided with a period of low oil prices caused by increased production from non-Persian Gulf sources, the political appeal of drawing down the US presence in the Gulf could grow and would be supported by those in the Democratic and Republican parties who believe that the United States is already militarily overextended.

Worst Cases and Best Choices*

Patrick Cronin

In the early 1990s, some observers warned that the energy relationships between Gulf and Asian countries might evolve into a potentially dangerous "Islamic-Confucian embrace." This played very effectively into two US nightmare scenarios: nuclear war in the Middle East and Chinese hegemony over Eurasia. Yet, these alarmist predictions, which were not based on rigorous analysis or empirical evidence, have not proved correct. From the US perspective, world energy market conditions are favorable and will remain so for the foreseeable future. This is due to several factors, including lower than expected energy consumption by Asian countries.

Energy Supply Security

There appears to be a consensus among energy analysts that world oil supplies are secure, and will remain so indefinitely. Not only is world oil demand growing at a slower pace than expected, but it is also shrinking relative to gas, which has become competitive for all end uses except transportation. Meanwhile, energy suppliers, particularly those in the Gulf, are eager to fill this growth in demand.

All Gulf countries are counting on significant increases in energy demand. Notwithstanding the slackening of Asian oil demand triggered by the financial crisis, Asia's developing countries (especially India and China) are expected to be the driving forces of future world energy demand growth. By the year 2020, taking into account the ill effects of the Asian financial crisis, energy consumption in developing Asia is projected to surpass by one-third that of all North America.

The current consensus is that the Asian financial crisis will bottom out in the next few years. However, the domestic problems faced by Asian countries are of such magnitude and complexity that no one can guarantee this will be the case. One must be skeptical about forecasts showing that, over time, Asian economies will attain high economic growth rates. An 8 percent growth rate for China, for example, seems unlikely, given the political, demographic, environmental and social challenges that lie

* This text is an edited version of the contributor's remarks made at the Middle East Institute's conference on "Gulf-Asia Energy Security" held at the Madison Hotel, Washington, DC, 9 July 1998.

ahead.

Yet, even if Asian economies do not duplicate the high growth rates they achieved in recent years, Asian energy demand will still be substantial. Although current per capita energy consumption in developing Asia is small compared to that of the industrialized world, this fraction will undoubtedly grow. Meanwhile, the Gulf, which has 65 percent of the world's proven oil reserves and enormous gas deposits, will serve as the major source of Asia's energy imports. New Gulf-Asia economic linkages will be forged, and energy trading between the countries of these regions will increase.

China (together with India) is the engine of future energy demand growth in developing Asia. Although most of China's imported oil will almost certainly come from the Gulf, China's efforts to "internationalize" its oil market since the mid-1990s has yielded impressive results. Indeed, China's energy picture is certainly brighter than security analysts had forecast several years ago. China's accomplishments suggest that the development of Gulf-Asia energy ties will not necessarily lead to disruptions and perturbations in the world energy market.

Potential US Policy Challenges

Looking to the future of Gulf-Asia relations, it is possible to sketch five scenarios in which oil might contribute to tension or even conflict. However, it is important to note that oil is only one independent variable. It could be an agent of indirect political influence in certain decision-making circles at different times.

1. Expanded Economic Competition

Increased Asian involvement in the Gulf and Central Asian energy markets need not be a source of tension. In fact, it might have a positive impact on the world energy market, and on economic growth in and bilateral relations between partners. The unexpected Chinese investment in Kazakhstan (to the exclusion of some Western interests) has, for example, the potential to yield these benefits.

2. Transportation of Oil as a Force-Building Justification

As increased amounts of oil flow from the Gulf, it will be imperative for the Chinese People's Liberation Army (PLA) to consider how to protect sea lanes and communications. These PLA concerns might serve as the justification for force buildups. Although this consideration alone might not lead to an arms race, it could contribute to similar measures by China's neighbors, if not by the United States. Therefore, the perceived need to "arm the oil road" could help drive domestic force structure debates and considerations in the Asia-Pacific region.

3. Arms-for-Oil Arrangements
Gulf-Asia energy relationships could lead to surreptitious arms-for-oil deals. These transactions—possibly including scientific and technical support for weapons of mass destruction programs in the Gulf—might occur beyond the control of Asian central governments. These dangers should not be exaggerated, nor should they be ignored.

4. Opposition to the US Role in the Gulf
China has not strongly supported the United States in the recent crises over Iraq. Furthermore, Chinese officials have consistently expressed their preference for non-military approaches to Gulf security. As China consolidates its energy relationships with Gulf countries, it might be even less likely than now to support United States positions in the United Nations on Gulf security issues. This could undermine the US role as "guarantor" of Gulf security and thereby place at risk the peace and stability of the region.

5. An Economic Depression in Asia
If an economic depression were to occur in Asia, the consequences would be dire for both the Asia-Pacific and Gulf regions. The perpetuation of the current Asian economic crisis, spurred by serious civil strife in some Asian countries or another round of major currency devaluations, could lead to depression. In turn, the fall off in Asian energy demand would further saturate the world oil market, resulting in even lower oil prices and lost revenues for Gulf producers. Under these circumstances, Asian and Gulf governments would be hard-pressed to maintain political control.

US Policy Opportunities
Worst-case scenarios aside, the development of Gulf-Asia energy ties presents more policy opportunities than dilemmas for the United States. In considering how to interpret and respond to Gulf-Asia energy ties, US officials could, and arguably should, factor them into a larger set of policy objectives. These objectives include ensuring the peaceful integration of developing Asia, particularly China, into a Pacific regional community and into international regimes. They also include fostering economic development in a new Middle East, a younger Middle East,

where demographics are changing rapidly and efforts to modernize and use information technologies are under way.

Conclusion

The development of Gulf-Asia energy ties might pose challenges, but certainly presents opportunities, for US policymakers. Looking to the future, it is important to emphasize that there are limits to what the United States can do to avert the dangers and exploit the potential of expanding Gulf-Asia energy ties. To the extent that the United States can help to maintain the stability of the global economy, including that of the Asia-Pacific financial market and the Gulf energy market, the United States itself will benefit. The United States, however, cannot accomplish this on its own. The United States should discuss, in bilateral and multi-lateral settings, its role as "guarantor" of Gulf security. The United States should initiate and conduct an "energy security dialogue" with China, Iran, the Arab Gulf states, and others. This might be not only prudent, but unavoidable. For, as the recent South Asian nuclear tests suggest, countries which have not had a central role in creating international regimes will increasingly insist upon a bigger stake in deciding the rules of the game. An energy security dialogue would highlight the need to think about the long-term issues of who will guarantee peace and how this responsibility can be and why it must be shared.

Appendix

Gulf-Asia Energy Ties*

Rilwanu Lukman

I am honored to be here today, and I would like to thank the organizers for their kind invitation and arrangements. This is a useful forum for exploring a very important topic: the growing energy ties between the Middle East and Asian regions. These two regions already dominate the global oil trade and this will continue and grow over the medium to longer term.

The energy trade between these two regions is largely one-way, with the Gulf supplying energy and Asia consuming it. It is certainly true that the Gulf has a net outflow of raw energy, and that Asia is the biggest consumer of that energy. But importantly, Asian investors, traders, operators and others are active in the energy sectors of the Gulf. On the other hand, Middle East companies and individuals have significant interests in the downstream energy industry in Asia. Without these relationships, the two regions could not expect to develop and grow such dynamic and robust trade in energy and other industries.

Despite the short term economic difficulties, Asia is expected to demand increasing amounts of energy over the medium to long term, and it is equally likely that the Gulf energy producers, particularly those in the oil and gas industries, will be the primary source of those energy supplies. This will ensure that the two regions develop ever-closer ties, not only in the energy industry, but also in other economic and social activities. While these relationships will be driven by mutual interests and market forces, they will also require considerable efforts by policymakers and others to overcome obstacles and support the growth of stable, trusting relationships. Allow me to elaborate a little on these points.

When we speak about Gulf energy, we are primarily referring to the petroleum industry of the Middle East. Oil constitutes not only the main source of energy in the Middle East, but also its largest source of energy exports. In fact oil is the largest source of Middle East exports in general, and thus it is of vital importance to the economies of this region.

Petroleum exports by OPEC Member Countries in the Middle East amounted to more than three-quarters of the value of their total exports in

* This text is a copy of Secretary-General Lukman's remarks made at the Middle East Institute's conference on "Gulf-Asia Energy Security" held at the Madison Hotel, Washington, DC, 9 July 1998.

1996. More than half of the oil exported by OPEC Member Countries in the Middle East went to Asia, representing 40 per cent of total OPEC oil exports. Clearly, therefore, Gulf petroleum producers are important to Asia not just due to their proximity, but also because of the Gulf's very strong petroleum production capacity and its considerable reserves.

The Gulf region's reliance on petroleum exports, and in particular on exports to Asia, is matched by Asia's strong reliance on petroleum imports from the Gulf.

As an oil-consuming region, Asia was the second largest behind North America in 1997, but it was by far the largest oil importing region, representing more than a third of total oil imports worldwide. Asia's oil imports equate to almost a third of its primary energy consumption. Importantly, the Middle East supplied around three-quarters of Asian oil imports and, therefore, 22 per cent of its primary energy needs.

I should note here that these figures understate OPEC's interest in the Asian region, since not only does OPEC have 6 Member Countries in the Middle East, but also one—Indonesia—within Asia. Indonesia, together with Malaysia and Brunei, is one of the major energy producers and suppliers within the Asian region and its gas exports in particular are growing strongly. Asia is experiencing a growing demand for natural gas, partly due to environmental concerns, and this will lead to stronger demand for gas imports, and this will benefit the Gulf.

In fact many Asian countries rely far more on imported oil and gas than does the region as a whole. The most obvious example is Japan, whose oil imports supply more than half of its primary energy needs. Again, the Gulf exporters play an important role in supplying these energy needs as the source of 77 per cent of Japan's oil imports in 1997.

Economy

Asia currently accounts for around a quarter of world oil demand, and this was expected to grow to 40 per cent of world demand by the year 2020. Asia was expected to represent 70 per cent of the expected growth in world oil demand between 1995 and 2020. Although those figures need to be reviewed in light of recent events and new economic forecasts, there is every reason to believe that Asia will continue to be a large and growing energy consumer and a major client for Gulf oil exporters.

Nobody can ignore the substantial currency devaluations and other adjustments that have followed years of rapid economic growth. Asia-Pacific primary energy consumption grew around three per cent in 1997, but the region as a whole is not expected to experience robust economic growth in 1998 and some countries are in deep recession. This should be reflected in lower short-term energy consumption overall. This is clearly an important concern for oil producers, particularly those in the Gulf.

Any reduction in oil demand in Japan or South Korea is keenly felt by in the Middle East, by OPEC and by oil producers in general. The Asian economic downturn is likely to impact on the global economy as a whole, and oil producers and consumers will both share the pain. No oil consumer or producer now operates in perfect isolation. Oil is traded around the world 24 hours a day, and events in one country can have an unforeseen impact elsewhere. But despite this interdependence, or perhaps because of it, there is a certain robustness to the global economy that can help to overcome weaknesses in a single country or region.

There are various predictions being made about the Asian Crisis and economists are still debating the long-term impact on other regions, and on Asia itself. As ever, OPEC is alert to these and other economic issues, and the Member Countries will continue to monitor events and respond as necessary in order to pursue their common interest in a stable and prosperous oil market. A good example of this was OPEC Member Countries' decision in June to cut their output for one year by 2.6 million barrels of oil per day from the level in February 1998.

OPEC Member Countries are also reaching independent agreements with non-OPEC oil producers who recognize that their cooperation and production restraint is in the common interests of producers and also consumers. By ensuring that the market receives sufficient oil supplies without becoming saturated, oil producers help to maintain prices at a reasonable level. In this way, they also help to ensure that the petroleum industry remains prosperous, and that should naturally support the necessary expansion of oil production capacity in line with the growth of demand.

And there can be no doubt that over the medium to long term the demand for energy and for oil will continue to grow, both globally and in Asia. Middle East oil producers will be at the forefront in meeting that demand and will need to continue developing their oil production capacity.

Asia's energy consumption per capita is well below that of the industrialized countries and significantly less than the global average. Therefore the region has substantial room for expansion and it can be expected to need increasing amounts of energy in line with its economic growth. Apart from economic growth, there are a number of other factors that could be seen either as opportunities or as potential obstacles to the development of the energy ties between the Gulf and Asia. In particular, I want to mention the environment, technology and information.

Environment

Perhaps the greatest challenge to the development of the global energy industry, and potentially to the improving energy ties between the Gulf and Asia is the emerging field of environmental policy. Coincidentally, the latest developments on this issue occurred in Kyoto, Japan at the Third Conference of Parties to the UN Framework Convention on Climate Change.

There has been a rapid development in environmental legislation, particularly taxation upon oil. As we all know, many industrialized countries are using taxes, particularly on oil, as a primarily tool to increase fiscal revenues. Many governments continue to justify such taxes in the name of environmental protection. As a result, fossil fuels, and especially oil, have been bearing an increasingly heavy tax burden. The oil consuming countries receive far more income from oil taxes than OPEC earns for its exports.

In 1996 the G-7 group of countries—Canada, France, Germany, Italy, Japan, the United Kingdom and the United States—levied around $270 billion of taxes on oil products. That was roughly twice as much as OPEC's net oil export revenues. Oil producers are simply not receiving a fair share of the economic rent from this limited natural resource.

At the retail level, end consumers in some countries are paying five times as much for oil products as the crude oil costs on the open market. Oil taxes represent 80 per cent of the price of gasoline at the pump in some countries, yet many consumers do not realize this. When gasoline prices rise, many motorists mistakenly blame oil producers instead of their own governments. When crude oil prices fall, few consumers rarely see a direct benefit because the price of crude oil is such a low proportion of the final price and because governments can raise their taxes to keep prices high.

By undermining energy demand, oil taxes threaten the long-term security of oil supplies. Oil taxes create considerable uncertainty about the likely development of economic growth and they reduce industrial competitiveness in those countries adopting them. Taxing oil is not a cost-free policy. It is not like taxing alcohol or cigarettes, the fiscal favorites. Because of the uniqueness of this product and the subsequent inelasticity of demand, consumers absorb a high level of oil taxes. But there will come a time when consumers can simply no longer afford these taxes, and that is when the industrialized countries will wake up to the true cost of levying this burden on the oil market.

If the governments of oil consuming countries really want to use taxes to reduce emissions of carbon dioxide, then it makes sense not to concentrate on oil, but to levy such taxes across all sources of carbon emissions. The OECD calculated that a pro rata energy tax, levied on all energy sources according to their carbon content, would maintain the OECD members' tax revenues, while reducing carbon dioxide emissions by 12 per cent from forecast levels by 2010. It is clear that simply changing the basis of the tax, by spreading it across all forms of energy rather than concentrating on oil, would benefit consumers and make it more equitable for producers.

OPEC Member Countries share the widespread concerns about the potential degradation of the environment, but we believe there are alternatives to the negative stance of industrialized countries that punishes both suppliers and users of fossil fuels, even to the detriment of their own economic development. It would be wise to develop a more positive stance towards this issue. Technology and investment can be usefully applied to the development of cleaner fuels and more efficient uses, such as the utilization of low-carbon fuels, efficient power generation and superior forms of insulation.

OPEC shares the concerns of countries that are likely to be strongly affected by the imposition of measures to reduce carbon emissions. Developing country oil exporters are especially dependent upon their oil revenues and any reduction in those revenues is of far higher significance to them than some industrialized countries may perceive, especially if it reduces our ability to develop our petroleum industries in line with demand. The result of such a scenario is the potential for shortages of petroleum supplies, and therefore price shocks that would be not only harmful for exporters and importers directly, but also harmful for the world economic system as a whole.

OPEC continues to pursue dialogue on these and other issues in bilateral and multilateral venues. Given the security of petroleum demand, OPEC has the reserves to ensure the long-term security of supplies. All petroleum producers share OPEC's concerns, and it is in their interests to support us. Likewise, oil consumers also benefit from a stable and prosperous petroleum market that offers them steady, reliable supplies.

Despite the obvious importance of climate change and the global environmental debate, Asian countries are more immediately troubled by issues of local pollution. As an example, emissions from coal steam power plants such as Nitrous Oxides and Sulphur Dioxides leading to acid rain can have a significant impact on agriculture and on the aquaculture industry which is a particularly important food resource in Asia. High atmospheric pollution is also a risk to public health, and this a particular problem in highly populated areas. India and China in particular are expanding their use of coal based power stations, due in large part to their relatively large domestic coal reserves and despite their potential for expanding hydro and nuclear power. Clearly, combined cycle power generation offers environmental advantages and, due to this and other environmental initiatives, we can expect Asia to make increasing use of natural gas, both from its own resources and from Gulf and other suppliers.

While local pollution continues to be the major immediate environmental concern in many parts of Asia, the global debate over climate change will also have a substantial impact on the energy sector in the region. For instance, Japan's efforts to reduce CO_2 emissions could increase its demand for gas, and this will likely be imported. Already, in the last decade Asia has become a net gas importer, and this has benefitted the Middle East. Interestingly for OPEC also, is the fact that Indonesia has become a growing supplier of gas, especially to Japan, South Korea and Taiwan.

Technology

Another means for addressing the issues of local pollution and global climate change is the development and exploitation of technology. This issue ranges from the use of tools to locate and develop new oil and gas reserves, to cleaner methods and processes of power generation, and greater efficiency in transport.

The petroleum industry has benefitted greatly from the development of such tools as 3-D and even 4-D seismic mapping, horizontal drilling and enhanced oil recovery techniques.

Technological developments are now very rapid. We know that anybody who has a technological advantage in the energy industry wants to exploit it as much as possible before that advantage is eroded by competitors. Therefore, it makes no sense to withhold technology from a particular contract or region, or even to demand greater compensation for its use.

Technology confers its own advantages, in terms of its ability to improve the location and recovery of oil and gas, to reduce the risk of accidents and waste, and to improve the development of cleaner fuels in the downstream. This saves both time and money, and all parties to these developments share in the benefits. As energy ties develop between the Gulf and Asia, we can expect to see greater cooperation in the development and exploitation of advanced technologies that tap into the significant resourcefulness of Asian countries and the substantial resources of the Gulf, whether in a technical sense or in other ways, for instance through the provision of investment capital.

Information

Another important issue that will affect the growing ties between Asia and the Gulf is that of information. We are entering an age where information has increasing importance and value, and yet also where more and more information is available. The rapid growth of the Internet and the sheer volume of financial and other data now flowing from specialized sources creates considerable challenges as well as opportunities. We need to ensure that we utilize information for its benefits and avoid becoming swamped with data. Certain types and sources of data may become a source of competitive advantage. There is also concern about the potential misuse or mistaken application of information. For instance, the volatility of financial markets can be exacerbated by a shortage of quality information, or by the deliberate leaking of facts or rumors. The development of energy ties between Asia and the Gulf will be greatly enhanced by the flow of reliable, timely information. When all parties are well informed they can more easily develop closer relations with fewer mistakes or misunderstandings.

I noted that the energy ties between the Gulf and Asia are of great importance to both regions, and that this importance is expected to grow in the medium to long term despite short term economic difficulties. I also noted the importance of these ties to OPEC, both in the Gulf and within Asia.

I also touched upon some of the major issues that will pose both obstacles and opportunities for the ties between the energy sectors in these two regions, including the environmental debate and related policies. I noted how energy taxes, particularly those on oil, can threaten the security of energy supplies by sapping the prosperity of the petroleum industry. I also mentioned the need for timely investment in the expansion of petroleum supplies and how this rests upon stable conditions in consuming countries and the equitable treatment of energy producers.

I also noted the need for the development and exploitation of technology and for the flow of quality, timely information between the Gulf and Asia.

In order to achieve progress in the face of these issues, the two regions will need to constantly monitor their energy ties with a view to building a deeper understanding of one-another's requirements. We need to appreciate the variety of views held by individual countries, investors and companies, and by the regions as a whole, as represented in the various trade blocs and other groupings of interest. Only in this way can we work together efficiently and effectively, with a common purpose and for our mutual benefit.

Ladies and gentlemen, thank you for your kind attention.

Issam Al-Chalabi

Al-Chalabi is a consultant based in Amman, Jordan. A mechanical engineer by profession, Al-Chalabi has served as president of the Iraq National Oil Company and as Iraq's minister of oil. He has participated in numerous conferences on world energy, regional cooperation, and political and economic development in the Middle East.

Fadhil Chalabi

Chalabi is the executive director of the Centre for Global Energy Studies in London. Chalabi served as director of Oil Affairs in Iraq's Ministry of Oil (1968) and as permanent under-secretary of oil (1973). In 1976, Chalabi held the position of assistant secretary-general of OPEC. His publications include *OPEC and the International Oil Industry: A Changing Structure* and *OPEC at the Crossroads*.

Patrick Cronin

Cronin joined the US Institute of Peace (USIP) in March 1998 as the director for research and studies. He is a specialist on peace and security issues in East Asia. Prior to joining USIP, Cronin was director of research at the National Defense University's Institute for National Strategic Studies (INSS). He helped to create *Joint Force Quarterly*, the professional military journal of the Chairman of the US Joint Chiefs of Staff. Cronin is the co-author and editor of the forthcoming book, *The US-Japan Security Alliances: Past, Present and Future*.

Sujit Dutta

Dutta is a senior fellow at the Institute for Defense Studies and Analysis (IDSA) in New Delhi. He is a specialist on Asia-Pacific security issues, especially China's foreign and defense policies. Dutta recently completed a period in residence as a senior fellow at the United States Institute of Peace. Previously, he represented India in the Working Group on Confidence and Security Building in the Asia-Pacific at the Council for Security Cooperation. Dutta has taught at the National Defense College, Foreign Service Training Institute, University of New Delhi, and Jawaharlal Nehru University. His publications include *China's Post-Mao Foreign Policy*.

Narsi Ghorban

Ghorban is director of the Iran Association for Energy Economics, of the International Institute for Caspian Studies, and of Asian Pacific, Inc. Over the past 19 years, as an independent energy consultant, Ghorban has worked with the Long Strategy Committee of OPEC, Mid-Continental Financial Services, Shell International, and the Institute for International Energy Studies. Ghorban has written widely on energy issues, particularly with regard to the Caspian Basin.

Yang Guang

Guang is managing director of the Gulf Research Center and director-general of the Institute of West-Asian and African studies at the Chinese Academy of Social Sciences. Previously, he served at the Chinese Academy of Social Sciences as associate professor and senior research fellow. He has been a visiting scholar at the University of Wisconsin. Guang has written widely on Middle East energy and development issues.

Geoffrey Kemp

Kemp is director of regional strategic programs at the Nixon Center for Peace and Freedom. During the Reagan administration, he was special assistant to the President and senior director for Near East and South Asian Affairs at the National Security Council. He is the author and co-author of several books on the Middle East, including, most recently, *Point of No Return: The Deadly Struggle for Middle East Peace* and, with Robert Harkavy, *Strategic Geography and the Changing Middle East*.

Rilwanu Lukman

HE Lukman is secretary-general of OPEC. During his distinguished career, he has served as Nigeria's federal minister of Petroleum Resources and as chairman of the Nigerian National Petroleum Corporation (1986); federal minister of Foreign Affairs, Nigeria (1989); chairman, Europe Energy Environment Ltd., London (1991); and chairman, National Electricity and Power Authority, Lagos (1993). Lukman has been awarded the Knight of the British Empire (KBE) and the Legion d'Honneur, as well as honorary degrees from the Universities of Bologna, London and Ahmadu.

John Mitchell

Mitchell is chairman of the energy and environmental program at the Royal Institute of International Affairs (RIIA) in London. In addition, he is research advisor to the Oxford Institute of Energy Studies and honorary fellow at the Centre for Petroleum and Mineral Law and Policy at Dundee University. From 1966-93, Mitchell held a number of positions at British Petroleum (BP), including special advisor to the Managing Directors and head of the *BP Policy Review* staff. Mitchell's major publications include *The New Geopolitics of Energy* (1996), which he edited, and *An Oil Agenda for Europe?* (1994), co-authored with S. Peake.

Katsuhiko Suetsugu

Suetsugu is director of the Asia-Pacific Energy Forum (APEF) in Tokyo. Since 1984, he has been a member of the Energy Policy Council of the Government of Japan. For the past three years, Suetsugu has also been a member of the Council on Official Development Aid of the Japanese Ministry of International Trade and Industry. During his career, he has served as an award-winning writer, columnist and Honorary Associate of *The Nikkei*. He was a research fellow in East Asian studies at Harvard University (1977-78), and a fellow at Harvard's Center of Business and Government (1994). Suetsugu's major publications include *Energy Reform* (1994).